Ancient Times

Ancient Times

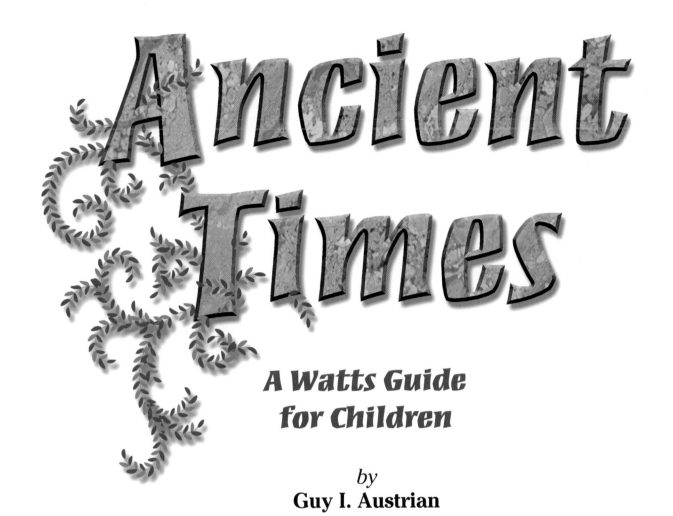

A Watts Guide for Children

by
Guy I. Austrian

FRANKLIN WATTS
A Division of Grolier Publishing
NEW YORK • LONDON • HONG KONG • SYDNEY
DANBURY, CONNECTICUT

Consultant: Anne L. Seltzer, English Department
The Peddie School, Hightstown, New Jersey

Developed for Franklin Watts by Visual Education Corporation, Princeton, New Jersey

For Franklin Watts
Senior Editor: Douglas Hill

For Visual Education
Project Director: Jewel G. Moulthrop
Editorial Assistant: Joseph Ziegler
Copyediting Supervisor: Maureen Ryan Pancza
Photo Research: Sara Matthews
Production Supervisor: William A. Murray
Interior and Cover Design: Maxson Crandall
Electronic Preparation: Fiona Torphy
Electronic Production: Rob Ehlers, Lisa Evans-Skopas, Isabelle Ulsh

Library of Congress Cataloging-in-Publication Data
Austrian Guy
    Ancient Times : a Watts guide for children / by Guy Austrian; consultant, Anne Seltzer.
        p. cm.— (Watts guides)
    "Developed for Franklin Watts by Visual Education Corporation, Princeton, New Jersey"—P.
    Includes bibliographical references and index.
    Summary: Alphabetically arranged articles present information about the ancient world, covering events, people, and practices around the world from prehistoric times to 500 A.D. and treating such topics as architecture, politics, family life, and religion.
    ISBN 0-531-11731-6 (lib. bdg.)   0-531-16550-7 (pbk.)
    1. Civilization, Ancient—Juvenile literature.   [1. Civilization, Ancient— Encyclopedias.]   I. Franklin Watts, Inc. II. Visual Education Corporation. III. Title. IV. Series.

CB311 .A87 2000
930 — dc21   99-057816

To the Reader

The world covered in *Ancient Times: A Watts Guide for Children* stretches around the globe—from Asia to Mesopotamia and from the Mediterranean to the Americas. Nearly 3,000 years separate the rise of the early societies in Mesopotamia and Egypt from the great and powerful Roman Empire. Although these civilizations seem remote to us today, much of our world has been shaped by the ideas, languages, literature, and customs of the ancient world. In fact, it is difficult to find a modern idea, invention, or field of study that does not have some basis in the ancient world.

In making this book, we have tried to highlight the people and events that may, perhaps, influence your life. You will find articles about the origins of alphabets and calendars. Other articles tell about the beginnings of medicine and astronomy. Some articles contain special features in small boxes. Most articles end with "See also" references. These cross-references point to related articles in the book.

There are many colorful pictures and photographs to help you imagine this world of long ago. You may notice some words in SMALL CAPITAL LETTERS. These words are defined in the Glossary at the back of the book. If you enjoy this book, and we think you will, turn to the back, where you will find a list of other books about the ancient world.

Throughout the preparation of *Ancient Times,* we have tried to highlight daily life as well as heroic events, and to keep the role of women in the ancient world a visible part of history. We also made sure to include the important contributions of civilizations that have sometimes been overlooked.

Finally, we decided to use the B.C. and A.D. styles for years and dates to make the stories and events easier to understand. This style, which is used by many people throughout the world, counts years before and after the birth of Jesus. (B.C. stands for "before Christ" and A.D. for *anno Domini,* which means "in the year of the Lord," or after Christ.)

I am especially indebted to Jewel Moulthrop for her commitment to the project, to Guy Austrian for his meticulous writing, and to my grandmother, who made me believe that reading Homer was one of life's great privileges.

Anne L. Seltzer
Hightstown, NJ

Abraham

Abraham is respected and revered as the founder of the Israelite nation. His life and faith began the history of three religions.

Abraham was born about 4,000 years ago. According to the Bible, God commanded Abraham to move to Canaan (present-day Israel), where he would become the founder of a great nation. In Canaan Abraham prospered and raised a family with two sons, Ishmael and Isaac.

The Bible tells how God tested Abraham's faith. In one instance, God instructed Abraham to sacrifice his young son Isaac on an altar. Abraham prepared to make the sacrifice. But God was only testing Abraham's willingness to obey. Just as Abraham was about to sacrifice Isaac, God stopped the killing and allowed a ram to be sacrificed instead.

Isaac grew up to have children of his own, including Jacob, whose sons are believed to be the ancestors of the ancient Israelites. Today, Jews recognize Abraham as the founder of Judaism. They believe that he was the first person to worship a single god rather than many gods. Christians also honor Abraham as their forefather. Muslims believe that Abraham's son Ishmael was the ancestor of the Arab people.

Aeneid

The *Aeneid* is an EPIC poem written in Latin by the Roman poet Virgil around 20 B.C. The form and style of this long poem are modeled on the *Iliad* by Homer, the great epic poet of Greece. The *Iliad* tells part of the story of the Trojan War, at the end of which Greek armies conquer the city of Troy. The *Aeneid* tells a story that begins after that war, as the Trojan hero Aeneas and a small band of his followers flee from the burning city.

After Aeneas leaves Troy, a storm blows his ship across the Mediterranean Sea to Carthage, a city on the coast of North Africa. Aeneas has a love affair with Dido, the queen of Carthage, but leaves her to continue his journey to Italy. Abandoned and heartbroken, Dido curses Aeneas and swears that Carthage will forever be the enemy of his people.

When the Trojans arrive in Latium, in western Italy, they meet the Latins. Aeneas defeats their champion in hand-to-hand combat and marries their princess, joining the two peoples. Virgil's aim was not only to write a poetic history but also to comment on the Roman world in which he lived. When Aeneas visits the underworld, for example, he meets his father, who tells him about the future and advises him on how the Romans should rule their future empire. In this episode and others, Virgil emphasized themes of peace, order, and responsibility.

Agriculture

Agriculture is the growing of crops and the raising of farm animals. Until around 8000 B.C., people found food by hunting animals and gathering wild plants. Gradually they learned to plant seeds and wait for the plants to grow. They also began to DOMESTICATE animals.

True agriculture began after 7000 B.C. People learned to choose the best seeds and to put them in the ground, using primitive plows or digging sticks. The first agricultural societies developed in river valleys with moderate amounts of rain. Farmers later learned to control the flow of water to their fields, a process called irrigation. When the rivers flooded, canals carried water to the crops. When the rivers returned to normal, dams kept the floodwaters in the fields. Still later, people invented machines, such as waterwheels, that could lift water from low-lying streams to higher farmlands.

Along the Tigris and Euphrates rivers in the Fertile Crescent of Mesopotamia, people grew wheat and barley and raised camels, donkeys, and horses. In India water from the Indus River was used to irrigate the rice, cotton, tea, and sugarcane plants. Indian farmers often used water buffalo for labor. In China fruits were commonly grown along the banks of the Huang He. There the ancient Chinese tended orange, pear, and peach trees.

By 2500 B.C., agriculture had been established in the Americas. There the most important food was maize, a type of corn. Other crops included beans, squash, avocado, and tobacco. In the Andes, the mountain range that runs up the west coast of South America, people cut terraces, or steps, into the hillsides to create flat land for fields. (See also *Food and Drink; Law; Science and Technology; Slaves and Slavery.*)

Life in ancient Egypt depended on water from the Nile. As farmers learned to control the annual flooding of the river, settlements developed along the river banks. This farmer is using a shadoof to irrigate his fields.

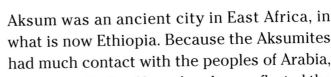

Aksum

Aksum was an ancient city in East Africa, in what is now Ethiopia. Because the Aksumites had much contact with the peoples of Arabia, particularly the ancient kingdom of Sheba, Aksum's culture reflected the traditions of other civilizations.

From about A.D. 100, the city was the capital of a small but wealthy empire that was also called Aksum. The Aksumites' prosperity came largely from trade. They bought goods, such as ivory, from other African kingdoms and then sold them to the peoples of Arabia, North Africa, and even faraway India. The Aksumites decorated their capital with impressive monuments, including carved stone towers—one was over 100 feet tall. Greek and Roman writings contain many accounts of Aksumite wealth.

In the early A.D. 300s, two Christians were shipwrecked on the shores of Aksum. They were taken prisoner but later rose to become honored officials in the Aksumite court. Eventually they succeeded in converting the country to Christianity. Aksum remained a Christian stronghold when Muslim Arabs conquered North Africa 400 years later. Today some Ethiopians believe that one of their churches contains the tablets of the Ten Commandments. They say that a son of King Solomon of Israel and the Queen of Sheba, whose meeting is described in the Bible, brought the tablets to Aksum.

Alaric

Alaric was the leader of the Visigoths, a Germanic people who attacked the Roman Empire in the early A.D. 400s. Born around A.D. 370, Alaric joined the Roman army as a paid soldier, as did many Visigoths. At the age of 25, however, Alaric led a rebellion against the Romans and was named king of the Visigoths.

Alaric posed a serious threat to the Roman Empire. Tensions ran high between the Eastern Roman Empire and the Western Roman Empire. When Alaric invaded Greece, the eastern emperor in Constantinople gave him Illyria, a region just east of Italy, in return for halting the invasion of Greece. From Illyria the Visigoths could easily invade Italy.

In 410, Alaric and his armies overran Rome, causing great damage. It was the first time in 800 years that enemy troops had invaded the IMPERIAL city.

The Visigoths did not remain in Rome but instead marched through southern Italy. Alaric died while making plans to cross the Mediterranean Sea and invade Africa. The Visigoths abandoned their leader's plans and headed north, back through Italy. The Romans allowed them to set up a kingdom in western Gaul (present-day France) and Spain. (See also *Attila the Hun.*)

Alexander the Great

Alexander III was a towering figure in the ancient world. Born in 356 B.C., he grew up in Macedonia, north of Greece. His father, King Philip II, wanted Alexander to have the best training, so he sent for the great teacher Aristotle, who came from Greece to tutor Alexander in science, geography, literature, and other subjects.

As a young boy, Alexander proved his talent as an athlete and a horseman. When he was only 12, he tamed a wild stallion named Bucephalus that none of his father's men could control. Alexander approached the spirited animal carefully and spoke to it gently. The sound of Alexander's voice had a calming effect on the horse, and from then on, Bucephalus was his.

Alexander was only 20 when his father was murdered and he became king. He began to build his empire by marching south into Greece. He completely destroyed the city of Thebes, and the rest of Greece quickly surrendered. Adding Greek soldiers to his army, the young king turned eastward toward his greatest enemy, Darius III of Persia.

In a series of stunning victories, Alexander shattered the Persian armies in the Middle East and Mesopotamia. Wherever he went, he spread the Greek culture he had learned about from Aristotle. He founded great cities that later became important centers of Greek learning.

Five years after becoming king, Alexander defeated the Persian Empire. But he was not content. He pushed his armies farther east, into unexplored lands. Fighting fierce tribes along the way, he marched his soldiers to the foot of the Hindu Kush mountain range. Beyond these towering peaks lay India, a mysterious land known to the Macedonians for its spices, jewels, and elephants.

Alexander's armies won spectacular victories in India. His soldiers were homesick, however, and refused to go farther east. Alexander gave in and agreed to begin the long march home. Many died from hunger and thirst on the journey through the Persian deserts. Alexander himself became ill and died at the age of 32. His generals and relatives quarreled over who would succeed him and his empire was soon divided. But Greek civilization had taken root in the regions Alexander had conquered. (See also *Philosophy, Western.*)

This mosaic shows Alexander the Great riding into battle on the back of his beloved horse, Bucephalus.

Alphabets and Writing

An alphabet is a set of letters or characters that represent the sounds of a spoken language. These signs are arranged in combinations to form words. The first writing systems started when prehistoric and ancient civilizations used pictures and characters to communicate and to keep records. The ancient Greeks developed the first modern alphabet by using separate signs for consonants and vowels. The Greek alphabet became the basis for many later alphabets, including those of Latin and English.

The earliest forms of writing were pictures, which were used to represent objects or ideas. Over time, these pictures came to resemble the original objects less and less. They began to represent the words for those objects, not the objects themselves. This important shift from pictures to words happened in at least seven ancient languages, including Sumerian, Egyptian, and Chinese. By 3000 B.C., the Sumerian language was written in cuneiform, a type of writing in which small, wedge-shaped signs were pressed into clay tablets. At about the same time, the Egyptians created a set of hieroglyphs, characters that represented objects, ideas, or sounds. By 1500 B.C., the Chinese language had its own set of about 3,000 characters.

Another important change in the development of alphabets occurred when people began to use signs to represent syllables—the combinations of consonants and vowels that form parts of words. Four such writing systems developed among the peoples who lived and traded around the eastern Mediterranean Sea, including the Phoenicians. In about the 800s B.C., the Greeks adopted the Phoenician writing system and made one important change—from syllables to single sounds. Instead of using signs that combined consonants and vowels, they used a separate sign for each consonant and each vowel. This was the first modern alphabet.

The Greek alphabet spread to the Etruscans of central Italy, who passed it along to the Romans. With the expansion of the Roman Empire, the Roman alphabet spread throughout Europe. It is this alphabet, which is also called the Latin alphabet, that is used for many modern European languages, including English, German, Swedish, Italian, French, Spanish, Polish, and Hungarian.

Other writing systems—mainly of the hieroglyphic type—developed in other parts of the world. For example, in the Americas, the Zapotec people had a system of picture writing from about 500 B.C., and the Maya used both pictures and syllables from about A.D. 300. (See also *Literature; Schools.*)

Antonine Emperors

The Antonine emperors were skilled leaders who governed the Roman Empire at the height of its power. The first was Trajan, who became emperor in A.D. 98. He had a strong sense of justice, and worked to improve the lives of Rome's poor people. His armies brought Roman rule to Eastern Europe and Arabia, and he insisted that conquered peoples be treated fairly. Trajan was called the "best of rulers."

After Trajan's death in 117, his relative Hadrian became emperor. Although Hadrian had the support of the army, many other people disliked him, including the senators. Hadrian ended Trajan's expansion of the empire; instead he focused his attention on maintaining peace and securing the frontiers of the empire.

With no major wars to fight, Hadrian had plenty of money to spend on large buildings, temples, and monuments. When he died in 138, the senators declared him a god, as they did other successful emperors.

To provide a barrier against invasion, the emperor Hadrian built a wall on the northern frontier of the Roman province of Britain. As shown here, parts of the wall are still standing.

Hadrian's adopted son, Antoninus Pius, also pursued peace, reform, and construction. He ruled over a secure and wealthy empire from 138 to his death in 161, when his own adopted son, Marcus Aurelius, became emperor.

During Marcus Aurelius's reign, the empire was attacked on its frontiers in Spain, Britain, and Asia Minor. While spending long years in army camps, Marcus Aurelius found time to keep a personal diary, which he called "Notes to Himself." He wrote about the heavy responsibility of being emperor. He followed a PHILOSOPHY called Stoicism, which said that people should accept what life brings.

Marcus Aurelius died in 180. He was the last of the great Antonine emperors. His son Commodus became emperor, but his cruel, wasteful behavior offended many people. His advisers arranged for a wrestler to strangle him during a wrestling match in 192. (See also *Germanic Peoples; Philosophy, Western.*)

Archaeology

Archaeology is the study of the physical remains of the past in order to learn about the lives and customs of people. Archaeologists search for and examine the remains of buildings, burial grounds, household items, artworks, and other objects. When studying cultures that had no written language, such as that of the Olmecs of Mexico, archaeologists rely on objects or pieces of objects. Where writing did exist, as in Egypt, archaeologists have learned much from ancient historians and record keepers—after they deciphered the ancient writings.

Archaeology became a field of study in the 1500s, when Europeans renewed their interest in the ancient world. The first major EXCAVATIONS took place around Rome; the goal was to find works of art that could be sold to collectors. The art and architecture that was discovered greatly influenced European culture. Many artists and architects drew inspiration from the ancient finds.

During the 1700s, archaeology became more scientific. Archaeologists developed specific tools and techniques to ensure that their work was accurate, precise, and reliable. They dug carefully with delicate shovels and brushes, taking detailed notes all the while. They learned never to move an object before recording its exact location and giving the object a number for identification.

The 1700s also marked the beginning of a "golden age" of archaeology. As European empires expanded to the far corners of the world, archaeologists gained access to thousands of sites. The buried Roman city of Pompeii, the mazelike palace on the island of Crete, an Inca city high on a cliff in Peru, the ruins of the city of Zimbabwe in Africa, the lavish tomb of the pharaoh Tutankhamen (King Tut) in Egypt—all of these discoveries, and many more, captured the attention of the world in the 1700s, 1800s, and 1900s.

The Buried City

One morning in A.D. 79, the citizens of Pompeii (in southwestern Italy) heard a deafening explosion. Mount Vesuvius, the volcano that towered over their city, had erupted. Within two days, Pompeii and neighboring villages were buried under tons of ash, rock, and lava. More than 2,000 people perished in the disaster.

The site lay abandoned for centuries, until workers digging an underground water line in the 1500s found the ruins. From 1738 to 1756, archaeologists carefully uncovered streets, shops, homes, gardens, sculptures, and paintings. What emerged was the world's most richly detailed view of an ancient city's life—and death.

One famous archaeologist was Heinrich Schliemann of Germany. He studied descriptions of Troy in Homer's *Iliad* and became convinced that he could find the ruins of the ancient city. Many historians doubted that Troy even existed. They believed it was only a legend. But in the 1870s, digging deep into a hill in Turkey, Schliemann discovered the city and learned a great deal about its culture. Clues in Homer's works also led Schliemann to the royal tombs of another ancient people—the Mycenaeans.

In the 1900s, archaeology transformed itself with new TECHNOLOGIES and approaches. New laboratory tools enabled archaeologists to determine the age of an object. Skeletons, in particular, yielded new information about what people ate, what diseases affected them, and much more.

Today important archaeological finds include not only artworks and buildings but also clothing, toys, and even garbage. As they expand their field, modern archaeologists rely on the knowledge of many other scientists—experts on plants, animals, rocks, medicine, agriculture, commerce, and other aspects of civilizations and their environments. Although no amount of information can form a truly complete picture of ancient life, archaeology helps us to understand societies of long ago.

When Mount Vesuvius erupted in A.D. 79, the Roman city of Pompeii was buried under volcanic ash. The ash preserved Pompeii's buildings and people.The ash cooled and became hard before many of the victims' bodies had decayed. This photograph shows plaster casts made from hollows formed by bodies of the victims.

Architecture is the art of planning and designing buildings. Although many of today's architects design houses, schools, and office buildings, ancient architects primarily designed and built monuments, palaces, and public buildings.

One of the earliest architectural achievements was the mastaba—a tomb for an ancient Egyptian pharaoh. A mastaba was a squarish mound with a brick or stone face, built over an underground room—the burial chamber. The design of the mastaba itself had several rooms, including a chapel and a secret room that contained a statue of the dead ruler. By about 2600 B.C., the design of the mastaba had evolved into a larger structure—a step pyramid that looked like a stack of mastabas, each a little smaller than the one beneath it.

The Colosseum (below) is considered one of the greatest architectural achievements of the Romans. It was used as a stadium for gladiator fights and held about 45,000 people— more than New York City's Madison Square Garden.

In Mesopotamia (present-day Iraq), builders used mud bricks to construct their buildings. Sometimes they added an outer layer of colorful GLAZED bricks for decoration. For very large buildings, they constructed brick platforms. By adding more and more layers of bricks, they built tall, terraced temples called ziggurats. The Persians adopted this style and added columns to their important buildings.

The Greeks, influenced by Persian architecture, developed graceful columns to support their open, boxlike temples. Greek architects developed three orders, or styles, of columns. The Doric column, which appeared in the early 500s B.C., is the simplest of the three orders. The Ionic column, which appeared around 570 B.C., is more slender and ORNATE than the Doric column. The third order, called Corinthian, developed in the late 400s B.C. It is the most ornate and was a favorite of the Romans.

The Greeks were among the first city planners, designing their cities around a large central marketplace called an agora. The most important building in any Greek city was its temple. In Athens, the Parthenon—the temple to the goddess Athena—is an example of the finest elements of Greek architecture, including its Doric columns.

The Hole in the Roof

The Pantheon in Rome is a temple to all the Roman gods. Many historians regard it as the ancient world's finest building. Its dome measures 140 feet across. It also has a large hole, called an oculus, at the top.

The emperor Hadrian included the oculus in his design when he started construction on the Pantheon in about A.D. 118. Statues of the gods lined the circular inside wall. As the sun moved across the sky, a beam of light shined on each god and goddess in turn.

The Romans were quick to adopt the principles and styles of Greek architecture. Roman architects used Corinthian columns in their most important buildings and monuments. At the height of the Roman Empire, builders imported marble from QUARRIES throughout the Mediterranean region. Roman builders excelled in TECHNOLOGY. They invented concrete—a mixture of stone fragments and mortar—and perfected the arch. These achievements enabled Romans to construct larger buildings, some with impressive domed roofs. They built bridges, public baths, AQUEDUCTS, and huge stadiums for gladiator games and other spectacles.

The Roman architect Vitruvius once said that architecture should have "utility, firmness, and delight." What he meant was that buildings should serve their purpose, be technically sound and stable, and have a pleasing appearance.

Armies and Warfare

War was a frequent occurrence during ancient times. Wars were generally fought to protect land, to gain more land, and to enslave conquered peoples or demand ransom of them. The earliest armies were often only a few dozen tribesmen strong. For centuries soldiers fought their enemies man-to-man. But by the 600s B.C., Greek armies had become more organized. Greek soldiers fought in tight units called phalanxes. A single phalanx consisted of eight rows of soldiers carrying shields and spears. These men advanced as a single force. The phalanx formation succeeded for hundreds of years, but men on foot were no match for the swift and powerful horsemen of Alexander the Great, who attacked Greece in 335 B.C.

In the ancient world, navies were less important than armies. At first, military boats were used only to transport soldiers. The Greeks were among the first to build ships for warfare. Some Greek ships were designed to ram enemy vessels and sink them.

The Romans also focused on land troops. They realized that the phalanx had some limitations. It was difficult for soldiers in a tight formation to move quickly across a battlefield. In the 300s B.C., the Romans replaced the phalanx with a unit called the legion. A legion had between 4,000 and 6,000 men who were organized into many smaller groups. Commanders could quickly and easily change a group's purpose or direction in battle.

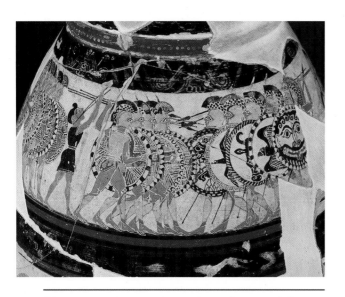

This painted vase shows heavily armed Greek foot soldiers known as hoplites. The hoplites are in a phalanx—a battle formation in which soldiers armed with spears and shields lined up shoulder to shoulder in groups of eight.

At first the Roman army was composed of citizens who left their farms or businesses to serve as soldiers whenever Rome was threatened. But as the Romans expanded their empire, their armies became both permanent and professional. Soldiers did not go home after a battle. Instead they stayed in their camps and received a salary for their service.

Eventually, however, the Roman armies became too widely scattered, and the soldiers' loyalty to Rome decreased. In addition, generals began to hire many non-Roman soldiers, who felt no loyalty to Rome. By the late A.D. 400s, Germanic armies from northern Europe had little trouble defeating the weakened and disorganized Roman legions.

Armor and Weapons

Armor is a protective covering that a person wears or carries for defense against weapons. Makers of weapons tried to produce arms that would penetrate the armor worn by most soldiers. Therefore, the development of armor and of weapons were closely linked.

The earliest weapons were sticks and stones. People fashioned wood into clubs. They threw stones or hurled them from slings made of animal hides. Early humans also found that certain types of rock, such as flint, could be split or broken into sharp pieces and used as blades for spears, knives, and arrows. These warriors protected themselves with armor made of wood, leather, or thick plant fibers.

Between 4000 and 3000 B.C., people learned to mold and sharpen metals such as bronze and iron. The use of metals gave rise to new weapons, including swords, and to new types of body armor. A typical ancient Greek foot soldier often carried a spear and a short sword. The Greeks wore helmets, chest armor, and shin guards, usually made of bronze or iron.

Although the Romans invented few new types of weapons and armor, they adapted and improved many existing items. They also developed methods for using them with the greatest force, accuracy, and effect. They were among the first to use armor made of MAIL and, later, of large iron plates. Ancient villagers protected themselves by building walls around their communities. This in turn led to new types of weaponry designed to destroy those walls. For example, catapults were invented. Their long arms were pulled back and released to launch boulders.

In the A.D. 400s, the Norse of northern Europe discovered startling new methods of making swords from iron. These weapons were the hardest, sharpest, and strongest the world had yet seen, and they were used for the next 1,000 years. (See also *Alexander the Great; Armies and Warfare; China; Germanic Peoples.*)

In the 200s B.C., the Chinese developed sturdy saddles based on the soft ones used in central Asia. With the addition of stirrups for his feet, a soldier could ride a horse while wielding a sword or throwing a spear.

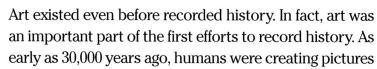

Art existed even before recorded history. In fact, art was an important part of the first efforts to record history. As early as 30,000 years ago, humans were creating pictures of the world around them. Some of these images have been found on the walls of caves in Spain and southern France.

Most ancient artists created objects and paintings to remember important people and events, to use in religious ceremonies, to display wealth and power, and to express their ideals of beauty. The art of many ancient cultures began with small figures of DEITIES, people, animals, and everyday objects. These items were shaped from clay, stone, wood, or ivory, and they often had religious importance.

Ancient Egypt, which flourished from about 3000 to 1000 B.C., developed an especially strong artistic style. Egyptian rulers, called pharaohs, had large tombs built for themselves. ARTISANS decorated the walls of these royal tombs with murals and reliefs—a type of sculpture carved into a flat surface. These decorations often showed scenes from the life of the ruler.

Greek artists painted on a variety of surfaces, including walls, wood panels, stone pillars, tombs, and pottery. Historians have learned much about Greek life from the paintings on their pottery, which show scenes from daily life as well as from MYTHOLOGY. Greek art was widely reproduced and its styles copied. In fact, much of what is known about Greek art has come from Roman copies of Greek sculptures.

Roman artists also developed several techniques of their own. The Romans created many beautiful murals in a style now called trompe l'oeil, which means "trick the eye." In this style, an illusion is created by painting a building or a distant landscape as if seen through a window or an open door.

Ancient art often depicted scenes from important ceremonies and rituals. This fresco, created by the Minoan people from the Greek island of Crete, shows a ritual in which men and women leaped over a charging bull.

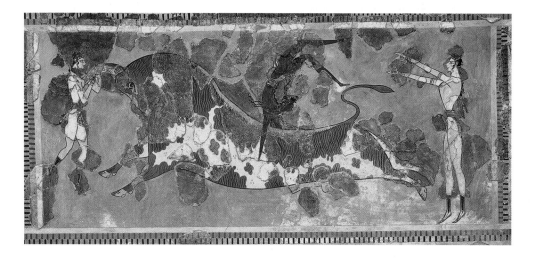

Assyrian Empire

The Assyrians lived in northern Mesopotamia (present-day Iraq). Their empire marked the last and greatest period of the ancient civilization called Ashur.

Until about 2000 B.C., the Assyrians were ruled by kings from the south. During the next few centuries, they experienced brief periods of independence but frequently were conquered by more powerful neighbors, including King Hammurabi of Babylon. One Assyrian ruler, Tukulti-Ninurta I, enjoyed a period of glory after his army captured Babylon in the 1200s B.C. Although the Assyrians were unable to hold the city for long, the event inspired later generations.

These winged bulls with human heads guarded the palace of an Assyrian king. Their ferocious appearance was believed to scare off evil spirits.

Assyria rose in power and influence in the 800s B.C., when it conquered hostile neighbors in the north. In the 700s B.C., King Tiglath-pileser III reorganized Assyrian society to ensure his power over other nobles and officials. He also led victorious armies into the great cities of Babylon and Damascus. His invasion of Samaria, the land of the northern Israelites, was completed by Sargon II, who forced all the Samarian Jews to move to Assyria. Under Sargon the Assyrian Empire dominated the Fertile Crescent. In the 600s B.C., the Assyrians even conquered distant Egypt.

Today the ruins of the Assyrian capital at Nineveh provide a wealth of information about the empire at its height. Assyrian ARTISANS also created long, elaborate wall carvings showing events in the empire's history, from great battles to lion hunts. Some carvings and CUNEIFORM tablets depict the achievements of the Assyrian armies. The Assyrians gained a reputation for terrible cruelty among the peoples they conquered. They frequently uprooted whole populations and brought them to Assyria, using their forced labor to enrich the empire.

But no empire is indestructible. A civil war and other revolts in the middle 600s B.C. weakened the empire. By 600 B.C. the great King Nebuchadnezzar II had completely defeated the Assyrians.

Astronomy is the scientific study of planets, stars, and other objects in the sky. Astrology is a set of ancient beliefs—not a science—about how the movements of these heavenly bodies affect human life.

People have always been interested in the heavens and in stargazing. Ancient peoples eventually came to recognize patterns and cycles in the way heavenly bodies moved across the sky. From these patterns they created systems of timekeeping—calendars to help them know when to plant and harvest their crops.

The Babylonians were among the greatest astronomers of the ancient world. By observing the sky, their skilled mathematicians could predict the future positions of the planets and stars with a high degree of accuracy.

Later the ancient Greeks described the arrangement of the universe. At first, Greek astronomers believed that the earth was at the center of a complicated system of circles and spheres. Then, around 270 B.C., the Greek astronomer and mathematician Aristarchus announced that the sun, not the earth, was at the center. Since most astronomers at that time believed that the earth was stationary, they rejected Aristarchus's claim. It would be 1,800 years before his ideas were proven to be correct.

Like many ancient peoples, the Maya of Mexico and Central America believed that the movements of stars, planets, and other heavenly bodies influenced their daily lives. This Mayan building was constructed so that its narrow windows aligned with various heavenly bodies.

People of ancient times also believed that there was a mysterious connection between heaven and earth. They were deeply interested in the heavens because they believed that the heavenly bodies influenced their lives. For this reason, many astronomers were also astrologers. In ancient times, astrology was used mainly for casting horoscopes, a form of fortune-telling. Based on the positions of the planets and the stars at the time of a person's birth, the horoscope was believed to show the pattern of that person's life.

As Christianity spread in the Roman Empire, astrology declined. The Christian Church banned fortune-telling, and in A.D. 357, the emperor Constantius II made it a crime punishable by death. Astrology was revived many centuries later, and today some people believe that it can be used to predict the future. (See also *Agriculture.*)

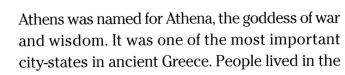

Athens

Athens was named for Athena, the goddess of war and wisdom. It was one of the most important city-states in ancient Greece. People lived in the region as early as 3000 B.C. By 1200 B.C., the Athenians had built protective walls around the center of the city. During this period, Greece was dominated by the Mycenaean civilization, centered in the city of Mycenae. Between 1100 B.C. and 950 B.C., however, invaders known as Dorians destroyed Mycenaean civilization and plunged Athens and Greece into a dark age.

About 200 years later, Athens and the surrounding villages were united as a kingdom. But several generations of rule by nobles led to unrest among the lower classes, who led very difficult lives. For decades, conflicts raged over which form of government the city should have. Around 508 B.C., a citizen named Cleisthenes rose to power and established an early form of democracy, enabling all citizens to participate in government. In the following years, Athenians strengthened and expanded their democratic form of government, which became a model for other Greek cities.

At about the same time, Athens became involved in a long struggle against Persia, to the east. Athens and its allies triumphed, completely defeating the Persians in the Battle of Marathon in 490 B.C. Athens eventually came to control much of Greece. Between 460 and 429 B.C., its economy grew, and democracy and culture flourished under the great Athenian leader Pericles.

However, the success Athens enjoyed did not last. The city's growing power led to conflict with other city-states, especially Sparta. Over the course of 55 years, two Peloponnesian Wars pitted Athens and its allies against the Peloponnesian League, led by Sparta. The second war ended in 404 B.C. with the defeat of Athens. Soon after that, all of Greece fell to King Philip II of Macedonia.

Although Athens had lost its political and military power, it remained a great cultural and educational center for some time. However, when Athens later came under Roman rule, the cities of Rome, Alexandria, and later Constantinople replaced Athens as the great capitals of the ancient world.

The religious center of Athens was located atop a hill called the Acropolis. This photograph shows the Acropolis and the ruins of the Parthenon, a temple dedicated to the goddess Athena.

Attila the Hun

Attila, born around A.D. 406, was the leader of a tribe known as the Huns. The Huns were nomads who traveled widely and were known for their fierce skill in warfare. Probably from the great plains and mountains of central Asia, the Huns conquered the Ostrogoths, Visigoths, and Vandals and forced these Germanic tribes westward into Roman lands.

When the brilliant and ruthless Attila became leader of the Huns in 434, his armies destroyed several major cities in the Eastern Roman Empire. The emperor had to pay Attila huge sums of gold to buy peace. In 450, Attila attacked the Western Roman Empire. The Roman general Aëtius gathered an army of Romans, Visigoths, and others and managed to turn back the invaders in Gaul (present-day France).

Attila died suddenly in 453. His two sons were unable to keep control of their European lands, and the Huns soon fell from power. However, Europeans never forgot Attila's terrible might, and his reputation for savagery still lives. (See also *Germanic Peoples.*)

Augustine

Augustine, a bishop who became a saint, was born in North Africa in A.D. 354. His mother was a Christian and his father was a PAGAN. As a young man, Augustine showed little interest in religion. He traveled to Carthage to study RHETORIC and then began a career as a teacher in North Africa and Italy.

While in Italy, Augustine heard the preaching of a bishop named Ambrose. The bishop preached that evil did not really exist as a separate force. He said that evil was simply the absence of good. Impressed by what he had heard, Augustine turned to Christianity and became a priest.

Augustine wrote about his religious conversion in his autobiography, which he called *Confessions*. He explained his struggle to change from a wild youth in search of pleasure to a mature adult in search of truth.

Saint Augustine is shown in this painting holding a shepherd's staff. The staff symbolizes his leadership and protection of Christians much like a shepherd and his flock.

Augustine established many of the philosophical principles of Christianity, such as the idea that God exists in the soul of every human being. His writings helped to strengthen Christianity during his lifetime and to preserve it as the dominant religion in Europe throughout the Middle Ages.

Augustus

Gaius Octavian (later called Augustus) was the first emperor of Rome. He was born in 63 B.C., and his great-uncle was Julius Caesar—the most powerful man in Rome.

In 44 B.C., Caesar was murdered by his enemies in the Roman Senate, who feared that he had grown too powerful. Octavian, Caesar's adopted heir, faced a strong rival for Caesar's power—Mark Antony, a trusted friend of Caesar's. The Senate supported the 18-year-old Octavian, hoping to be able to control him. With help from Caesar's loyal armies, Octavian defeated Antony's forces.

Octavian became consul (a high government official), but the Senate began to ignore him. He joined forces with his former rival Antony and Marcus Lepidus, another old friend of Caesar's. Together they marched their armies into Rome and forced the Senate to accept their rule. But this political alliance, called the Second Triumvirate, did not last long. When Lepidus supported a rebellious navy admiral, Octavian stripped him of power.

Meanwhile, Antony was living in Egypt with Queen Cleopatra. Octavian accused him of disloyalty to Rome and declared war on Egypt. In 31 B.C., he defeated Antony and Cleopatra's forces at Actium, in Greece, and chased them to Egypt.

In 31 B.C., Augustus became the first emperor of the Roman Empire. During his 45-year rule, he expanded the empire and began a long period of peace and prosperity known as the Pax Romana *(Roman Peace).*

Octavian was careful to act as though he were sharing power with the Senate. In reality, however, Octavian alone controlled the armies and the government. The Senate granted him many titles, including commander, first citizen, and high priest. They also named him Augustus, which means "revered one."

Augustus brought peace to Rome after years of civil war. He encouraged artists and poets and was responsible for many important building projects, including a network of roads that connected Rome with other parts of the empire.

The city of Babylon, in ancient Mesopotamia (present-day Iraq), was the center of two great empires. These Babylonian empires existed centuries apart. Both made remarkable advances in the fields of law and architecture.

Babylon, which means "Gate of God," was settled before 3000 B.C. At first the city was small and unimportant. Then, around 1900 B.C., the Amorites, a people from the north, conquered Babylon and several neighboring cities. Hammurabi, the Amorite king of Babylon, united all of Mesopotamia under his rule. His reign, which lasted from 1792 to 1750 B.C., was the peak of the first Babylonian Empire. A mighty conqueror and a careful ruler, Hammurabi is best known for his code of laws. He also encouraged Babylonian culture by supporting the work of artists and scholars.

Hammurabi's son was unable to maintain control of the empire after his father died. For the next 1,000 years, Babylonia was ruled mainly by foreign powers, including the Assyrians. In the 620s B.C., the Assyrian Empire came under attack from the Medes. The Babylonians revolted and reestablished their independence. They were led by the Chaldeans.

Chief among the kings of the Chaldean DYNASTY was Nebuchadnezzar II, who ruled from 605 to 562 B.C. During his reign, Babylon became one of the greatest cities of the ancient world. It had a larger population than any other city in the region. It was home to the spectacular Hanging Gardens—one of the so-called Seven Wonders of the Ancient World. The Babylonians were also skilled mathematicians and astronomers. Babylonian artists created impressive decorations on palace walls, and people used CUNEIFORM writing to mark clay tablets in several languages.

For all its greatness, Babylon fell to the Persians less than 25 years after Nebuchadnezzar II died. A series of foreign rulers followed. Their capitals were in other cities, and Babylon's greatness faded. Today the ruins of the city can be seen about 50 miles south of Baghdad, the capital of Iraq. (See also *Law.*)

This bull, made of colored glazed brick, decorated an avenue called the Processional Way, which led to the ancient city of Babylon. Each year, Babylonians carried statues of their gods down the avenue to celebrate the new year.

Buddhism

Buddhism is a religion that began in India about 2,500 years ago. At that time, India was changing as many people left the countryside to live in towns and cities. Many new ideas rose to compete with traditional Hindu beliefs, and of these, Buddhism gained the widest acceptance.

Buddhism is based on the teachings of the prince Siddhartha Gautama. He was known to his followers as the Buddha, meaning "Wise One." Buddha is neither a supreme god nor the creator of the Universe. He taught that all beings have desires they cannot fulfill and that they suffer because of this. He said that people could escape suffering through discipline, MEDITATION, and faith and by following a path to enlightenment—a state of wisdom and peacefulness called nirvana.

After Buddha's death in about 480 B.C., his followers formed communities of monks and nuns who studied his ideas and taught them to local people. Their relationship with the people was based on the Buddhist idea of giving. Because the monks and nuns lived in poverty, people gave them food and clothing. In return the people received instruction on how to live a Buddhist life. Buddhist monks and nuns normally did not marry or have children. It was common for a family to send at least one child to be raised and educated to become a monk or a nun.

The Indian emperor Asoka was an important early supporter of Buddhism. In the 200s B.C. he made Buddhism the official religion of his empire and sent his own son and others to spread the religion to India's neighbors. Asoka also held a large gathering of Buddhists to debate their different understandings of Buddha's teachings. One group that emerged, the Theravada (Way of the Elders), taught that only certain people, such as monks, could achieve enlightenment. Another group, the Mahayana (Great Vehicle), taught that enlightenment was available to all.

As Indian culture spread throughout Asia, so did Buddhism. When Buddhist teachers arrived in a new land, they often sought the support of local rulers, and many gained positions of great respect in the royal palaces. With the support of kings, they set up Buddhist communities in many countries—Burma, Thailand, Indonesia, Sri Lanka, Nepal, Korea, China, and Japan. People often combined Buddhism with their traditional beliefs and practices. By the Middle Ages, Buddhism was one of the world's major religions. Since the mid-1900s, there has been a renewed interest in Buddhism. Today Buddhism plays an important role in the spiritual and cultural lives of more than 300 million people. (See also *Christianity; Islam; Hinduism; Judaism.*)

Born in 100 B.C., Gaius Julius Caesar came from the Julii family. Although the Julii were nobles, they had little wealth or political influence. In 84 B.C., Caesar married Cornelia, the daughter of an important citizen who had opposed Sulla, the tyrant of Rome. Sulla ordered him to divorce Cornelia, but Caesar left the city instead and joined the military. There he gained a reputation for his courage and leadership.

After Sulla's death, Caesar returned to Rome and entered politics. He often disagreed with members of the Roman Senate, who he felt were not governing in the people's interest. Popular with the people, Caesar was elected to several important government posts.

In 60 B.C., with the support of Pompey (a talented general) and Crassus (a wealthy politician), Caesar became consul, the highest official in Rome. The three men formed a political alliance and tried to undo some of the harm that Sulla had done to Rome and its citizens. Caesar spent the years between 59 and 50 B.C. conquering Gaul (present-day France) in what became known as the Gallic Wars. During that time, however, Crassus was killed in battle, and the Senate persuaded Pompey to turn against Caesar.

In 49 B.C., the Senate, fearing Caesar's growing popularity with his soldiers, ordered him to return to Rome or face charges of treason. Caesar tried to work out a compromise with the senators. When they rejected his offers, he marched his armies into Italy, beginning a civil war between his forces and those of Pompey. After pursuing and defeating Pompey's armies in Spain, Greece, Egypt, and North Africa, Caesar returned to Rome in triumph.

By 46 B.C., Caesar was the most powerful man in Rome. Many in the Senate still regarded him as a threat to the REPUBLIC. On March 15 (the Ides of March), 44 B.C., a group of senators, including his friend Brutus, surrounded Caesar on the floor of the Senate and stabbed him 23 times. (See also *Augustus; Cleopatra; Julio-Claudian Emperors.*)

Crossing the Rubicon

When the Senate ordered Caesar to return to Rome without his army, he instead marched his troops across the river Rubicon —toward Rome. The expression "crossing the Rubicon" has come to mean choosing a course of action from which there is no turning back.

Julius Caesar was very popular among ordinary Romans. But some Roman senators regarded him as a threat to their power and they stabbed him to death.

Calendars

Since ancient times, people have used calendars to keep track of the days, weeks, and months in a year. By 2000 B.C., several cultures had learned how to arrange large stones to track the movements of the sun, moon, stars, and planets across the skies. The knowledge they gained helped them to plan for such seasonal tasks as planting and harvesting.

Arrangements of stones, however, are not really calendars because they do not organize the year into regular periods of time. But like most calendars, these stone markers were based on observations of the movements of objects in the skies. Also, like all calendars, they had a similar purpose—to plan for holidays and seasonal events, such as the rainy season.

Most early calendars were divided into months, periods based on the phases of the moon. A new month began when people saw a new, curve-shaped crescent moon. Since the moon's cycle takes 29½ days, most months were 29 or 30 days long. However, 12 LUNAR cycles (months) fall 11 days short of a full year. This meant that calendars fell out of step with the seasons every few years. To fix the problem, an extra month was added every few years. Most ancient societies used this type of calendar—in Mesopotamia, Egypt, Greece, Rome, China, India, and elsewhere. One exception was the Maya in Central America. They used an 18-month calendar in which each month had 20 days.

The ancient Roman calendar did not correctly mark the time it takes for the earth to make one complete trip around the sun. Therefore, it did not accurately predict the arrival of the seasons. For example, by the time Julius Caesar became dictator of Rome in 49 B.C., winter began in September on the Roman calendar. Caesar and the Greek astronomer Sosigenes created a new calendar that added one day in every fourth year—the leap year. Known as the Julian Calendar, it is still in use, with only minor corrections. (See also *Astronomy and Astrology; Feasts and Festivals.*)

Egyptian Water Clocks

While calendars measure the passage of days, months, and years, clocks are needed to account for smaller periods of time. In about 1400 B.C., the Egyptians created a timekeeping instrument called a water clock. They punched a small hole at the bottom of a bowl and filled the bowl with water. As the water dripped out, marks inscribed on the inside of the bowl were exposed. These marks showed how many hours had passed since the bowl had been filled with water. Water clocks remained the most accurate timepieces in the world until the invention of mechanical clocks thousands of years later.

Carthage

The Phoenicians were an ancient people whose capital city was Tyre (in present-day Lebanon). They founded the city of Carthage in North Africa around 814 B.C. Its excellent harbor and its location on the Mediterranean coast made it ideal for trading. The city grew quickly in size and wealth until it dominated the western Mediterranean and had many colonies of its own.

In the 600s B.C., Tyre came under attack from the Babylonians and the Persians, and Carthage became an independent city-state. Carthage's power brought it into conflict with the Greeks, who also had trade routes and colonies in the Mediterranean region. Carthage fought several wars with Greek city-states, often over the large island of Sicily.

As Rome's power rose during the 400s and 300s B.C., Carthage first became an ally of Rome. By the 200s, however, Rome's ambitions clashed with those of Carthage. The two cities fought three wars known as the Punic Wars.

The second of these wars featured the daring strategy of the Carthaginian general Hannibal. With an army and a special force of battle-trained elephants, Hannibal crossed the Alps and invaded Italy. He fought there for 16 years before returning to Carthage to defend the city. Carthage survived, but it lost much of its territory in Spain and Africa.

During the reign of the emperor Augustus (from 31 B.C. to A.D. 14), Rome built a new city on the same site. The new Carthage had grand public buildings, including a stadium and public baths. Carthage grew rapidly, and by A.D. 100, it was a center of trade, Roman culture, and Christianity. In 439, the Vandals, a Germanic tribe, made it their capital. In the mid-500s, it was part of the Eastern Roman Empire, and in the 600s, Carthage was conquered by the Arabs. (See also *Germanic Peoples.*)

The great Carthaginian general Hannibal is best known for his daring feat of marching his army—and 38 elephants— across the Alps into Italy.

China

The Chinese civilization that began along the banks of the Huang He, or Yellow River, was one of the first highly developed societies in the world. The ancient Chinese created a system of writing, metalworking techniques, and sophisticated calendars.

Around 400 B.C., the region entered a time of conflict that historians call the Period of Warring States. As the small states struggled to survive, power was given to men according to their talents and ability rather than their wealth and social class.

The Han dynasty lasted for more than 400 years and reached its peak under the emperor Wudi. This painting shows the Han palace on a spring morning.

Order was restored in the 220s B.C., when the Chin state gained control over the other states. The Chin ruler named himself Shi Huangdi, meaning "First Emperor." The emperor and his highest official, Li Si, supported the idea that strict laws and severe punishments were the best way to rule. With the emperor's approval, Li Si decreed that everyone must use the same system of writing and of measurement.

Meanwhile, Shi Huangdi tried to protect his territory. He had his builders join several existing walls in the north to form the Great Wall of China. This kept northern tribes from invading. To pay for the wall, high taxes were levied on the people. Unhappiness with the emperor's harsh government grew, and the Chinese people rebelled.

The Han DYNASTY came to power in 202 B.C. Although the Han also established a strong central government, they had more concern for the well-being of their citizens. The Han dynasty reached its greatest power during the 52-year rule of Han Wudi. His conquests in western Asia gave China control of the Silk Road, a major trade route across Asia to the Roman world. Chinese civilization flourished under the Han. Paper and porcelain were invented, and poets created a unique tradition of Chinese literature.

Weakened by political power struggles, the Han dynasty fell to rebellious peasants in A.D. 220. China became divided; for more than 700 years, its kingdoms were ruled by a series of short-lived dynasties. (See also *Philosophy, Eastern.*)

Christianity

Christianity is a religion that began in the first century A.D.—the early days of the Roman Empire. The first Christians were a small group of people who followed the teachings of Jesus, a Jew from Nazareth (in present-day Israel). In fewer than 400 years, Christianity had become the official religion of the Roman Empire.

After Jesus died, in about A.D. 30, his followers wrote several accounts of his life and teachings. Some of them worked to spread these teachings. As the number of believers increased, they formed communities in many cities. At first they met in private homes. But as the number of Christians continued to rise, they soon built places of worship, called churches.

The writings about Jesus were collected into a book that became known as the New Testament and served as the basis of this new religion. Christians believe that Jesus was the son of God and that he died and then rose from the dead to save all human beings from punishment for their sins. However, the early Christians had many disagreements among themselves. Some groups, such as the Copts of Egypt, established their own versions of Christianity.

The night before Jesus was crucified, he met with his disciples for a meal, which came to be called the Last Supper. Today, Christians share bread and wine in a church ritual called the Eucharist or Holy Communion, which symbolizes their spiritual connection with Christ.

Roman officials regarded the early Christians with suspicion and disapproval. Around A.D. 63, the emperor Nero began the practice of executing Christians by feeding them to lions. During the 200s and early 300s, the Romans tried to end Christianity by burning churches and arresting priests. The situation improved for Christians in 313, when the emperor Constantine issued an EDICT of tolerance for all religions. In 391 the emperor Theodosius made Christianity the official religion of the Roman Empire. When the empire split into eastern and western sections in 395, the Christian Church began to split as well. The western Roman Catholic Church was led by the bishop of Rome, known as the pope. The Eastern Orthodox Church was led by the bishop of Constantinople, known as the patriarch.

Both churches grew ever stronger. When the Western Roman Empire fell in 476, the Roman Catholic Church survived and became the leading religion of Europe during the Middle Ages. (See also *Judaism.*)

City-States

In ancient times, a city-state was an independent city and the territory under its control. That territory could be the surrounding villages and farms, or it could include more distant regions, such as land that had been colonized. As these settlements grew in size and importance, ancient peoples began to identify more with their city-states than with their tribes.

City-states often shared cultures, languages, and even borders with their neighbors, but they fought fiercely to preserve their independence. People honored the founders of their city-states with festivals and holidays. Most city-states were identified with a particular god or goddess, who the people believed would protect them in times of trouble.

When war or other disaster struck, the people from outlying areas moved into the central city for protection. Because government buildings were located in the central city, people gathered there to participate in public life. Most cities had large open areas that served as gathering places for merchants, politicians, entertainers, and others. City-states often formed alliances with neighboring city-states for protection from common enemies and to increase control over trade. (See also *Athens; Rome; Sparta.*)

Cleopatra

Cleopatra was born in 69 B.C. She inherited the throne of Egypt from her father when she was only 18 years old. A highly intelligent and ambitious woman, Cleopatra reluctantly shared power with her two younger brothers until one drowned as he fled from battle; the other was killed by her order.

This sculpture is one of the few portraits believed to show what Cleopatra really looked like.

Cleopatra formed alliances with two of the most powerful men in Rome—Julius Caesar and, later, Mark Antony. In 44 B.C., Caesar was murdered by his political enemies, and Cleopatra became involved in the struggle for power that followed his death. Cleopatra supported Mark Antony.

Antony decided to live in Egypt with Cleopatra. They planned to create a new empire together. Antony's rival, Gaius Octavian, persuaded the Romans that Antony was no longer loyal to Rome and declared war on him. In 31 B.C., Octavian's navy defeated the fleet of Antony and Cleopatra at the Battle of Actium in Greece. Unwilling to become Octavian's prisoner, Cleopatra retreated to Egypt and killed herself by allowing a poisonous snake to bite her. (See also *Augustus.*)

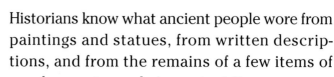

Clothing

Historians know what ancient people wore from paintings and statues, from written descriptions, and from the remains of a few items of clothing. The clothes worn by most people in ancient times were remarkably simple and changed very little over time.

In Egypt's hot desert climate, people wore loose garments made of linen in its natural light color. Men wore cloths around their waists—waistcloths—and sometimes capes on their shoulders. Later, waistcloths became longer and were pleated. Women often wore linen tunics that hung from their shoulders to their ankles. The Egyptians decorated themselves with belts, collars, headdresses, jewelry, black wigs, and dark eye makeup.

As the empires of Mesopotamia (present-day Iraq) changed, so did the clothing styles of the people who lived in the region. The Sumerians wore leather skirts or woolen robes. They walked barefoot and shaved their heads. The Babylonians, on the other hand, favored long tunics and fringed robes. The Assyrians added more details, such as tassels and embroidery. Assyrian men wore their hair and beards long and curled, and women wore headbands of leather or gemstones.

Fashions from Mesopotamia and Persia (present-day Iran) influenced early Greek clothing styles. But after defeating an invasion by the Persians in the early 400s B.C., the Greeks avoided eastern styles and wore simpler clothes. A man usually wore a waistcloth under a long rectangular garment that was fastened at the shoulders and waist. Greek women wore long tunics.

In Rome, a man most commonly wore a toga—a single large piece of cloth draped and folded around the body. Most togas were plain, but some were embroidered or dyed according to the wearer's position in society. For example, because purple dye was the rarest and most expensive, only the emperor was allowed to wear purple clothing. Toward the end of the Roman Empire in the A.D. 400s, Romans adopted the styles of the invading Germanic tribes, including boots, pants, and shirts.

Ancient Mayan nobles wore headdresses made from colorful bird feathers and jewelry carved from jade and other gems.

Confucius

Born in 551 B.C., Confucius was an ancient thinker whose teachings about society, politics, and human relations greatly influenced Chinese civilization. He believed that rulers received their authority directly from heaven and that they were responsible for maintaining peace and order in their lands. Confucius proposed that people follow certain guidelines in their behavior toward one another. People who lived by these guidelines would serve as models for others, so that eventually everyone's behavior would be in harmony.

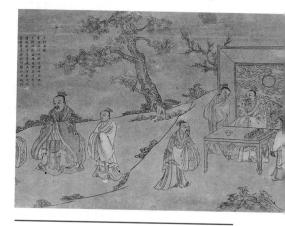

After Confucius died, his students collected his teachings into a book of sayings called the *Analects,* and his teaching came to be known as Confucianism. Under the Han DYNASTY, which ruled from 202 B.C. to A.D. 220, Confucianism was made an official part of Chinese law and culture. People who trained for positions in Chinese government were tested on their knowledge of Confucianism. The teachings of Confucius spread widely and were a major influence on Chinese culture and religion.

Confucius's real name was Kong Qiu. The name Confucius is from a title meaning "Great Master Kong." This illustration shows Confucius with some of his students.

Constantine I

Constantine I, the first Christian emperor of Rome, was born in Serbia around A.D. 280. On the eve of a battle with one of his rivals in 312, Constantine had a vision. He saw a cross in the sky with the words: "By this sign you shall conquer." Convinced that God was on his side, he ordered his soldiers to paint crosses on their shields. The next day, they won the fierce battle for control of Italy.

As the Roman emperor in the West, Constantine at first shared power with Licinius, who ruled the eastern part of the empire. Although he was tolerant of other religions, Constantine devoted himself to Christianity and encouraged his subjects to convert.

In 324, Constantine became sole ruler of Rome. He established his capital on the site of the ancient city of Byzantium (present-day Istanbul, Turkey). The city, renamed Constantinople, became a center of trade, learning, and religion. Constantine died in 337, leaving his sons to fight among themselves for control of the empire.

Crafts

Human beings have always sought the materials and developed the skills to produce the articles they needed. Prehistoric people discovered flint and bones for making weapons, clay for shaping pots and bowls, plant fibers to weave roof and floor coverings, and animal hides to fashion into shoes and armor.

As skills were improved and refined, the appearance of an item became as important as its function. With dyes made from plants and seashells, cotton and wool could be transformed into a variety of bright hues and woven into intricate patterns. Painters and engravers decorated their objects in many different ways. By the 500s B.C., Greek artists were painting works of art on vases and other pottery containers, including scenes from history, legends, and daily life.

New crafts arose as people learned to mine, smelt, and shape metals—especially bronze, tin, and iron—into a wide variety of items. Blacksmiths produced nails, tools, ploughs, armor, and weapons. As the skills of metalworkers improved, they began to make delicate jewelry in copper, gold, and silver. MINTING coins, a process developed in Asia Minor in the late 600s B.C., was another important metal craft.

Although there were some women craftsworkers, most were men. Fathers frequently trained their sons in a craft. Sometimes an entire family specialized in a particular craft. For example, most of the shipbuilders of the Athenian fleet were related to each other.

If a craftsman had no sons, he might take on a young assistant, called an apprentice. These boys spent several years helping the master with various chores while gradually learning the trade in hopes of becoming an expert craftsman.

Craftsworkers in rural areas often knew several trades. An armorer might need to prepare his own leather and forge his own buckles. Large cities, on the other hand, had enough craftsmen and customers to enable craftsworkers to specialize in a particular item, such as musical instruments.

Ancient peoples often associated specific crafts with specific gods and goddesses. For example, the Greek god Hephaestus—called Vulcan by the Romans—was associated with metalworking and was worshiped by Greek and Roman blacksmiths. (See also *Art; Clothing; Trade.*)

This painting on a cup, made in the 500s B.C., shows a craftsman making a helmet for a Greek soldier.

Darius I

Darius I ruled the Persian Empire from 522 B.C. to 486 B.C. He strengthened his hold on territories that Cyrus the Great had conquered in the mid-500s. He also completed Cyrus's political reforms by creating districts that were ruled by governors called satraps. Darius maintained close control by making frequent visits to the districts. An excellent system of roads enabled postal service workers and IMPERIAL messengers to travel quickly and deliver information to Darius about events in his vast empire. Darius was the first Persian ruler to MINT coins. Although Darius practiced the Zoroastrian faith, he showed great tolerance for the religions of the people he conquered.

In the midst of all the wealth and glory, however, trouble began in Asia Minor, which was part of the empire. Darius put down several rebellions there; then he accused the Greek city-state of Athens of supporting the rebels. Persian armies marched toward Athens, but the Greeks united against them. Darius was defeated at the Battle of Marathon in 490 B.C., but the conflict, known as the Persian Wars, continued under Darius's son Xerxes I.

King David

David, the son of a shepherd from Bethlehem, became the second king of ancient Israel. As a young man, David became the armor bearer for Saul, the first king of the Israelites. Saul had united the people in defense against the Philistines.

David gained fame when he fought Goliath, the gigantic Philistine champion, and brought him down using only a slingshot and a stone. He married Saul's daughter Michal, but his life at court soon became difficult. Saul began to experience fits of depression and took out his frustration on David. He even threatened to kill David.

David left Israel for several years, earning a living as a soldier. Meanwhile, Saul lost a battle against the Philistines and killed himself. In the struggle for power that followed, David returned to Israel and was named king of Judah, the southern part of the country. He soon became ruler of the entire kingdom.

David finally defeated the Philistines, ensuring Israel's independence. He also established Jerusalem as his capital. During his reign, which lasted from about 996 to 962 B.C., David pursued his interests in music and poetry, composing many PSALMS. However, in his later years, he was forced to flee Jerusalem when his son Absalom led a revolt against him. The conflict ended when another son, Solomon, was named David's heir. David died around 962 B.C. (See also *Judaism; Palestine.*)

Democracy

The word *democracy* comes from the Greek words for "rule of the people." Democracy is a form of government in which the people govern themselves.

The first democracies were established in ancient Greek cities, most notably Athens. When Cleisthenes came to power in Athens in about 508 B.C., he divided the population of the city-state into ten tribes. Each tribe chose 50 members by lottery to serve on the Council of 500. The council wrote laws and presented them to the citizens, who met in large gatherings called assemblies. The assembly then voted for or against each proposed law. Each citizen had one vote.

The assembly met about 40 times a year. Usually, around 6,000 citizens turned out for these outdoor meetings, which lasted several hours. In addition to voting on laws, the assembly elected judges to apply the laws and generals to command the army and navy.

Although this system sounds very democratic by present-day standards, Athenian democracy had some serious limits. Only free, adult males—or only one of every ten people—could be citizens. Women, children, slaves, and foreigners were barred from citizenship, and thus were unable to participate in government. Another limitation was that council members were not paid for their service. Therefore, although poor citizens were allowed to become council members, almost none could afford to take time from work to participate.

When the great Athenian leader Pericles came to power in the mid-400s B.C., he established a policy of paying council members so that poor citizens could serve. Pericles believed strongly that every citizen was important to the city and its government. But some Athenians disapproved of giving power to commoners. This view was expressed by the PHILOSOPHER Plato, who argued that only the most talented members of a society should govern it.

In the late 400s B.C., Athenian democracy declined after the city lost the Peloponnesian War against Sparta, which was not a democratic city-state. Athenian democracy was renewed in the mid-300s B.C., but it was soon forgotten when the army of King Philip II of Macedonia conquered Greece.

The ancient Romans showed some interest in Greek democracy. They formed councils called comitia. One such comitia, called the *Comitia Tributa,* was controlled by Rome's poorer people (called plebeians). But the comitia soon lost its power to the Senate, which was controlled by wealthy nobles (called patricians). Eventually all power rested with the Roman emperors, and democratic governments disappeared until the late Middle Ages.

Drama

Drama is the art of writing and performing plays for an audience. In ancient Greece, choruses—groups of dancers and singers—performed at religious festivals, playing heroes, kings, and queens as they acted out scenes from history and legend. Gradually, Greek drama became a specialized art form. By 500 B.C., it was of two main types: tragedy and comedy.

Tragedies described the hardships suffered by noble and heroic characters. Aeschylus wrote several tragedies, drawing on ancient myths to present such important issues as justice and duty. Another ancient Greek playwright, Sophocles, also tackled serious themes, but he focused more on the emotions of his characters. Euripides, a third Greek playwright, used his plays to show how people's weaknesses can lead to their own destruction. Greek audiences already knew the stories, so the playwright's task was to present the tales in new ways.

Writers of comedy usually created their own funny and improbable situations. In his comic plays, Aristophanes often poked fun at people in Greek society, from the great thinker Socrates to such common characters as a witless shepherd or a bossy wife.

Greek drama influenced Roman playwrights, but the Romans treated their plays with less respect. Roman drama was designed primarily to entertain, and comic plays were far more popular than tragic ones. The early Christians considered playacting IMMORAL, so when the Roman Empire officially converted to Christianity, the theaters were closed.

A different dramatic tradition developed in Asia. In the temples and royal courts of ancient India, actors spoke and sang on raised platforms with curtains, similar to today's stages. Early Chinese theater consisted mainly of MIMES and acrobats. Asian drama was often even less realistic and more symbolic than that of the Greeks and Romans. (See also *Literature; Music and Dance*.)

In ancient Greece, plays were performed in large outdoor theaters. Actors wore masks with exaggerated features to show their characters' feelings to the audience.

Eastern Roman Empire

In the late A.D. 200s, the Roman Empire began to split into two sections. While the Western Roman Empire declined and eventually collapsed, the Eastern Roman Empire became stronger and more powerful. The eastern section later came to be called the Byzantine Empire.

The Roman emperor Diocletian took the first steps toward this split by allowing assistants to rule different parts of the empire. After Diocletian ABDICATED in 305, a civil war raged for several years until Constantine I became emperor in the West and Licinius gained power in the East. In 324, Constantine defeated Licinius. Although Constantine became ruler of the entire empire, he shifted its center of power to the East.

He built a capital at the site of the ancient city of Byzantium (present-day Istanbul, Turkey). Originally named Nova Roma (New Rome), the city came to be called Constantinople in honor of the emperor. Constantine greatly expanded and developed his new city, erecting many monuments, statues, public buildings, churches, and a grand sports arena. He oversaw the construction of new walls that were strong enough to protect the city for centuries. Because Constantine had become a Christian, the city became a center of Christian culture. As in Rome, many people converted to Christianity. Unlike the Western Roman Empire, people in the East spoke and wrote in Greek, not Latin.

After Constantine's death in 337, a series of emperors struggled to control the two parts of the empire. The division between the eastern and western sections of the empire grew deeper. The government in the West was too weak and inefficient to resist invasions by Germanic armies and finally fell in 476.

Meanwhile, the Eastern Roman Empire also faced attacks from Germanic peoples, Huns, and Persians. However, Constantine's successors, such as Julian the Apostate, ensured that the empire would survive. They strengthened the position of the emperor and created an efficient government and a powerful army. Despite these improvements, life remained difficult for ordinary people, who were unable to change their positions in life. Farmers could not leave their land, and craftspeople could not change their jobs.

The Empress Theodora

Justinian and Theodora were married in 523, when he was a powerful prince and Theodora was a beautiful actress. Later, as emperor, Justinian relied greatly on Theodora. She was his most trusted adviser. She may even have saved her husband's reign. During a revolt against Justinian's rule, riots and fires erupted in Constantinople. Justinian considered fleeing the capital, but Theodora urged him to stay and take strong action against the rebels. He did, and remained in power for another 33 years.

This mosaic shows the emperor Justinian and his attendants—political advisors, church officials, and soldiers. Justinian kept invaders from the empire and built the magnificient Church of St. Sophia in Constantinople.

Like much of the empire's culture and government, the Christian Church was influenced by eastern ideas, ceremonies, and arts. The emperors worked to preserve eastern Christianity during bitter debates among Christians with differing beliefs. The Christian Church in the Eastern Roman Empire became known as the Eastern or Eastern Orthodox Church.

One of the greatest rulers of the Eastern Roman Empire was Justinian, who ruled in the mid-500s. A strong supporter of Christianity, he also reorganized Roman laws and reconquered much of the old Western Roman Empire. However, the wars of conquest in the West were very expensive, and Justinian forced his subjects to pay heavy taxes to cover the costs. Furthermore, the wars exhausted the empire's wealth and energy.

The rulers who followed Justinian were unable to hold onto territories in the West, but they strengthened the empire in the East. The Eastern Roman Empire prospered greatly and lasted until 1453, when Constantinople was conquered by the Turks. (See also *Attila the Hun; Rome.*)

Egypt

One of the first and greatest ancient civilizations arose along the Nile River in Egypt. Over time, people had settled in the Nile's narrow river valley because the land there was good for farming. Two kingdoms developed, one in the river's DELTA near the Mediterranean Sea and another farther south.

Around 3100 B.C., Menes, the ruler in the south, united the two kingdoms and governed from his capital at Memphis. The next 1,000 years (a period known as the Old Kingdom) were a time of great power and influence for the rulers of Egypt. The pharaohs, as they were called, maintained strict order in the kingdom, which became the model for later Egyptian rulers. Their godlike status was expressed in their enormous tombs—pyramids that seemed to reach to the sky.

By 2200 B.C., however, Egypt had become divided. Power rested with local rulers, who fought long wars against one another. Egypt was reunited around 2040 B.C. by Mentuhotep II, and a new era—the Middle Kingdom—began. The pharaohs worked hard to restore their power and influence and turned their attention to the needs of their people. A new middle class developed, and everyone was permitted to participate in the religious life of the community.

By 1800 B.C., high-ranking officials had become the power behind the thrones. Their internal struggles weakened the kingdom and it fell to invaders—Cushites from the south and Syrians from the northeast.

In 1570 B.C., a new DYNASTY ushered in the New Kingdom, during which Egypt flourished as never before. Strong, able pharaohs drove out invaders and enlarged the empire. By 1450 B.C., Egypt had conquered Ethiopia, Palestine, and Syria. Merchants and diplomats established contacts with other cultures, including the Babylonians, the Assyrians, and the Mycenaeans.

Built more than 4,500 years ago, the pyramids of Egypt required the labor of thousands of workers and slaves. Over 2 million blocks were used to build the Great Pyramid at Giza.

The pharaohs gave the job of running the empire to ministers, while they themselves toured the country to make inspections and to display their power. Religion was very important during this period, and priests became wealthy and influential. Although the priests were very powerful, they did not challenge the pharaohs, because the pharaohs were considered gods.

A period of decline began in 1150 B.C. Eventually Egypt was split into 11 separate kingdoms. This disunity enabled foreign powers—Nubians, Assyrians, and Persians—to invade Egypt. Although the pharaohs continued to rule, they were dominated by foreigners for centuries.

The Religious Revolution

Amenhotep IV, who changed his name to Akhenaton, ruled Egypt in the 1300s B.C. He is best remembered for his attempt to change Egyptian religion. When he became pharaoh, Egyptians believed in many gods. Akhenaton believed in one god and told his subjects that he himself was the earthly son of that god. His wife, Queen Nefertiti, also supported this new religion. Although the priests opposed Akhenaton, they were powerless while he lived. After his death, the priests restored the old belief in many gods.

In 332 B.C., Alexander the Great conquered Egypt, bringing Macedonian rule and Greek culture with him. At first the Egyptians welcomed Alexander for freeing them from Persian rule. But after a while, many Egyptians felt that they had traded one group of conquerors for another. After Alexander's death, his empire was divided. One of his generals, Ptolemy, took control of Egypt, establishing the Ptolemaic or Macedonian dynasty. After the death of Cleopatra—the last Macedonian ruler—in 30 B.C., Egypt became part of the Roman Empire. But when Rome split into eastern and western empires in A.D. 395, its control of Egypt began to weaken. In A.D. 642, Arab invaders conquered Egypt.

(See also *Archaeology; Gods and Goddesses; Mummies.*)

Families

The family is a basic unit of human society. The structures and traditions of families are even more varied than the cultures of the world. In most societies a family consists of one or two parents who care for children and raise them to be members of their community.

In ancient times, however, the family unit was not so simple. For example, in ancient India and Tibet, a woman could have more than one husband. In other parts of the world it was common for a man to have more than one wife.

Ancient households often included members of the extended family, which might include aunts, uncles, cousins, and grandparents.

In ancient Greece, men usually married at age 30—after they had completed their required military service. Although young girls might be promised in marriage when they were around 12, they did not marry until later. Husbands ruled their households, and wives were expected to produce male children to inherit the father's property and titles. In some Greek city-states, female children were abandoned.

In Rome, both the bride and the groom had to agree to the marriage. Girls could marry at 12, but a boy of 14 needed permission from his father to marry. Roman wives had more power and independence than Greek wives. The Roman emperor Augustus believed so strongly in the importance of family that he passed several laws to encourage people to marry and have children. One such law rewarded a man for each child he BEGAT by reducing the man's public service requirement by one year. (See also *Agriculture; Women.*)

Children were highly valued in Roman society. This sculpture shows scenes from a boy's childhood. He is nursed by his mother, held in his father's arms, and later given a chariot to drive.

Feasts and Festivals

Major holidays marked the times for planting crops and gathering harvests. New moons, flood seasons, and EQUINOXES also inspired religious activities. Ancient peoples saw natural events in terms of their own lives—winter symbolized death, and spring represented birth. In some cultures, this yearly cycle developed into a calendar, used to help people to keep track of regular holidays.

Gods and goddesses were frequently the focus of holidays. The Romans, for instance, held major festivals in March, which was named for Mars, the god of

This painting shows an elaborate Roman banquet. Such feasts usually consisted of many exotic foods—oysters and jellyfish for appetizers; roasted pig, duck, and rabbit for the main course; and pastries dripping with honey for dessert.

war. Priests danced with swords and shields to pray for the success of military campaigns in the spring. Like most ancient peoples, the Romans believed that gods played an active role in their lives. Many festivals were intended to honor, worship, and please a certain god or goddess and to bring good fortune to the people.

The city of Athens, for example, held an annual event called the Panathenaia to celebrate the birthday of Athena, the city's PATRON goddess. This spectacular festival included performances and contests in music, drama, poetry, and sports. Priests sacrificed many animals to the goddess, and Athenians feasted at grand banquets held in her honor.

Hospitality—the custom of hosting guests—was greatly valued in many ancient societies. Hosts offered their guests food, drink, conversation, entertainment, and even gifts. Wealthy and powerful individuals often held feasts to show their high social position. Sometimes the guests were political rivals, and the host would try to impress them with strange foods and lavish generosity. Petronius, a Roman writer and entertainment director for the emperor Nero, told the story of a lavish banquet in his work the *Satyricon.* Seeking to impress his guests, the host of the banquet serves an enormous roast pig. Just as the dish is carved, live birds flutter out of the cooked pig's belly, to the astonishment and delight of the guests. (See also *Olympic Games; Rituals and Sacrifices.*)

Fertile Crescent

The Fertile Crescent is a horn-shaped area in the Middle East. It stretches along the Mediterranean coast of present-day Egypt, Israel, Lebanon, and Syria; then it runs southeast between the Tigris and Euphrates rivers to the Persian Gulf. The region is called the Fertile Crescent because it receives more rain than the surrounding desert and dry plains.

The water and rich farmland in the Fertile Crescent enabled the farmers of ancient times to grow more food than they needed for themselves and their families. This extra food freed some people to do work other than farming. They built dikes to control the flooding of the Tigris and Euphrates rivers and dug canals to irrigate the land. These improvements enabled farmers to grow even more food and thus led to population growth. Some people built cities, where they settled and became craftsworkers, merchants, or government workers.

In the Fertile Crescent, Sumer (present-day southeastern Iraq) emerged about 8,000 years ago as one of the world's first city-based civilizations. Sumerian cities, such as Uruk, Lagash, and Ur, were surrounded by high, thick walls and held 5,000 to 10,000 people. The streets of these cities were narrow and crowded with people traveling on foot to buy food at the market or to offer sacrifices to their gods at the ziggurat—a pyramid with steps leading to a temple on the top. Most people lived in small houses made of mud and brick. Beneath many of these houses were tombs, where families buried their dead.

The Sumerians developed a counting system, based on the number 60, that is still used today to count hours and degrees on a compass. The Sumerians also invented a system of writing called CUNEIFORM. They were careful record keepers, and thousands of their clay tablets—covered with records of grain harvests, business debts, and other information—still exist.

The later history of the ancient Fertile Crescent includes larger and more powerful empires, including the Babylonian, Assyrian, and Persian empires. (See also *Alphabets and Writing; Jerusalem.*)

In the region of the Tigris and Euphrates rivers, the rich land of the Fertile Crescent curved around from the southeastern Mediterranean to the Persian Gulf.

Food and Drink

The earliest humans gathered wild berries, roots, and leaves, along with small animals, fish, and insects. The discovery of fire and the invention of pottery increased their choices of ways to cook. The development of agriculture, about 10,000 years ago, enabled ancient people to raise crops and animals for food.

The first diets based on agriculture consisted mostly of grains. In Europe and Africa, wheat and barley were common, while Asian societies depended more on rice and MILLET. Roots, such as potatoes and MANIOC, provided nutrition in the Americas. The cooking practices of prehistoric peoples were fairly simple. Meat and fish were typically grilled or roasted over an open fire. Grains were boiled or made into paste for bread.

The ancient Greeks and Romans ate many of the same foods. However, geography produced differences in their diets. For example, the Romans ate wheat and beef, while the Greeks ate more barley and fish. One reason was that Greece lacked grazing land for large herds of animals but had an abundance of fish and seafood.

Although the Greeks made cheese from goat's milk, dairy products were only a small part of their diet. Both the Greeks and the Romans cooked with olive oil, which was plentiful. Olives and grapes were among Greece's most important crops. Greeks and Romans, including their children, drank wine with almost every meal.

Alcoholic beverages, made from grapes or grains, were consumed in most ancient societies. In India, people brewed tea leaves in hot water, a practice that spread to China, Japan, and other parts of Asia. Coffee beans were used to make a popular hot drink in East Africa and Arabia. People in the Americas enjoyed a chocolate drink, similar to cocoa, but thicker.

In addition to chocolate, ancient American people cooked a wide variety of vegetables that were unknown on other continents. These included peppers, squash, gourds, tomatoes, and corn. It was the Chinese, however, who developed the ancient world's most spicy dishes. China had little wood for cooking fires, so the Chinese cut all their food into small pieces that cooked quickly. (See also *Feasts and Festivals.*)

Fish was an important part of the diet in ancient Greece. This painted vase shows a fishmonger cutting fresh fish for a customer.

Germanic Peoples

North of the Roman Empire, in the forested plains of Europe, people lived in villages, farming and hunting with other members of their clans. Beginning in the 500s B.C., some of these groups began to spread to the south and west. In the 300s B.C., they came into contact with the Romans, who called them Germans. The Romans also called these people Barbarians, a name that comes from the Greek word *barbaros,* meaning "foreign" or "ignorant." The word later referred to people who lived outside the Roman Empire, especially those hostile to Rome.

One of the earliest Germanic clans known to the Romans was that of the Gauls, who lived in what is now France. The Gauls invaded Italy and SACKED Rome in 390 B.C. They were soon driven out of the city, however, and by 51 B.C., the Romans had conquered all of Gaul and made it a Roman colony.

Another major Germanic people—the Goths—settled at the eastern edge of the Roman Empire near the Black Sea in the A.D. 100s. Later some Goths were forced westward by the Huns, a fierce people from Asia. In the late 300s, the Romans allowed the Visigoths (western Goths) to settle within the empire. This peace ended when the Visigoths invaded Italy and sacked Rome in 410. When their leader, Alaric, died, the Visigoths headed north through Gaul and into Spain, where they formed a new kingdom.

The Vandals were another Germanic people who had settled in Spain. However, the arrival of the Visigoths forced the Vandals southward into North Africa, where they established a kingdom in Carthage. In 455 the Vandals invaded Italy and sacked Rome before quickly returning to North Africa.

Shortly afterward, the Ostrogoths (eastern Goths) invaded Italy and seized control of Rome. In 476 the Ostrogoth leader Odoacer forced the last Roman emperor to give up the crown, marking the end of the Roman Empire. Odoacer became king of Italy. During his reign, he extended his territory to include the island of Sicily, which he took from the Vandals.

Not surprisingly, the Romans hated and feared the Germanic peoples. While admitting that the Germans were strong and skilled warriors, the Romans mocked their great height and lighter skin and believed that they were drunkards. Even so, the Germans adopted many of the Roman laws and customs, and most eventually converted to Christianity. The mixture of German and Roman cultures became characteristic of the nations that emerged during the Middle Ages. (See also *Alaric; Attila the Hun.*)

Gladiators

Gladiators were prisoners of war, slaves, or criminals in ancient Rome who fought each other in "games" that were held for public entertainment. Unlike the Greek games, which emphasized athletic skill, the Roman games featured blood and spectacle.

The first Roman gladiator games were held in 264 B.C. as part of the funeral for a wealthy man. Because the gladiator fights were so popular, they soon spread to occasions other than funerals.

People of all classes attended the games—from the poorest laborers to the emperor himself. Some gladiators fought against wild animals, but most fights were between two or more men. When a gladiator was defeated but still alive, members of the audience decided his fate by holding out their hands with thumbs pointing up or down. Thumbs up meant that the loser should be spared; thumbs down meant that he should die. The SPONSOR of the games usually went along with the decision of the crowd. Many spectators placed bets on the outcomes of the fights.

The emperor, high-ranking officials, or wealthy individuals sponsored the games. As a result, the games were partly political events. Sponsors competed with one another for the support of the public by staging the most expensive and most spectacular events possible. As the empire began to decline during the A.D. 300s, so did the popularity of the gladiator games.

Although many people attended and enjoyed the games, some Romans spoke out against them. Critics complained about the cruelty and danger faced by the gladiators. Others accused rulers of holding the games to distract the public from important issues. Once in a great while, the gladiators themselves rebelled. One famous revolt was led by a gladiator named Spartacus, who for two years defeated Roman armies in combat before dying in battle in 71 B.C. (See also *Olympic Games.*)

Gladiators fought until one gave up and asked for permission to leave the stadium alive, or until one or both died in the battle.

Gods and Goddesses

Ancient peoples worshiped many gods and goddesses who represented the various forces of the world. Groups of gods, called pantheons, usually included a few major DEITIES and dozens of lesser ones. The pantheon of a culture often changed over time as people were exposed to new ideas and adopted the deities of other societies.

One of the earliest known pantheons developed in Egypt before 3100 B.C. Like the gods found in most ancient MYTHOLOGY, the Egyptian gods were related to forces of nature. The Egyptian god Atum created the gods Shu and Tefnut, air and moisture. Next came Geb and Nut, the earth and sky gods, who produced four other gods—Osiris, Isis, Set, and Nepthys. Set, an evil god, killed Osiris. Osiris's son, Horus, killed Set in revenge. The Egyptians believed that Horus was their first king, or pharaoh. In later centuries, Egyptians also worshiped a supreme god named Ptah, who created the universe, and Amen-Ra—a combination of Amen, the god of the powerful city of Thebes, and Ra, the sun god.

Many societies had myths about the creation of the world. From 2000 to 1000 B.C., invaders from central Asia—called Aryans—spread throughout much of Europe, the Middle East, and western Asia, bringing stories of their gods with them. When they invaded Greece, they introduced their sky god, Dyaus, who later became the Greek god Zeus. Other major Greek gods included Poseidon (god of the sea), Hades (god of the underworld), Apollo (god of prophecy, healing, and music), Artemis (goddess of animals and hunting), Ares (god of war), Aphrodite (goddess of love), Hephaestus (god of fire and crafts), Hermes (messenger of the gods), Athena (goddess of wisdom, war, and art), and Demeter (goddess of fertility). Together with Zeus and his wife, Hera, these gods were known as the Twelve and formed the Greek pantheon.

However, these gods were not considered the first to have ruled the universe. Before them there were the Titans—the children of Uranus (sky) and Gaia (earth). Cronos and Rhea, the king and queen of the Titans, produced Zeus and other gods and goddesses. Afraid that his children would remove him from power, Cronos swallowed them at birth. When Zeus was born, however, Rhea gave Cronos a stone wrapped in baby's clothing. He swallowed the stone thinking

Hindu Divinities

In India the most important Hindu gods are Brahma, Vishnu, and Shiva. Together they form the Hindu pantheon called Trimurti. Brahma is said to have risen from a 1,000-petaled rose that grew out of Vishnu's navel. He later created the universe and everything in it. Brahma is the supreme god of the Hindu pantheon, Vishnu is the preserver, and Shiva is both the destroyer and the creator. Initially the Trimurti was worshiped as a single deity, but later, each god was worshiped separately. Brahma is rarely worshiped today, but Vishnu and Shiva still have large followings.

Poseidon is shown here driving his chariot and wielding his trident—the three-pronged spear he used to stop storms and cause earthquakes.

it was the baby. When Zeus grew up, he forced Cronos to release the children he had swallowed. Next, he and the other gods defeated the Titans and imprisoned them under the surface of the earth. Thereafter, Zeus was considered supreme by both gods and humans.

At first, the Romans worshiped three powerful gods: Jupiter (the supreme god), Mars (god of war and agriculture), and Quirinus (god of the Roman people). Most Roman gods were adopted from the Greek pantheon, but with different names. For example, Hera was known as Juno, Poseidon was known as Neptune, and Hades was known as Pluto. In fact, the Greek Twelve soon became the most important Roman gods. As their empire grew, the Romans began to worship the gods of the peoples they conquered and gave them Roman names. The Romans also worshiped their own emperors as deities and believed that emperors and some members of their families became gods when they died.

Not every ancient religion included a pantheon. Judaism and Christianity are MONOTHEISTIC. Ancient Christians and Jews believed in one god who was the creator of the universe and was all-powerful, all-knowing, and present at all places at all times. (See also *Buddhism; Hinduism; Myths and Legends; Underworld.*)

49

Greece

The civilization of ancient Greece had an immense influence on the western world—Europe, North Africa, and the Middle East. Ancient Greek ideas about education, politics, art, literature, and science still influence our lives. These ideas were spread by the conquerors of Greece, the Macedonians and especially the Romans, who admired Greek culture.

The first Greek-speaking people, called Mycenaeans, arrived in the Mediterranean region sometime before 2200 B.C. These early Greeks established a highly organized society ruled by kings and nobles. Warfare was an important part of their culture. They built palaces surrounded by thick walls to defend themselves against their enemies. Hundreds of years later, the Greek poet Homer told the legend of the Mycenaeans' war against the city of Troy in his famous EPIC poem the *Iliad*.

The Mycenaeans' power began to decline in the 1200s B.C. Soon afterward, another Greek-speaking people—the Dorians—seized control of the mainland and forced the Mycenaeans to move east across the Aegean Sea to Asia Minor. Although the two peoples were rivals, they believed in the same gods and goddesses and celebrated the same festivals. These shared gatherings helped create a sense of Greek unity.

The Dorians formed independent communities called city-states throughout Greece. Each city-state had its own laws and MINTED its own coins. These communities thrived and their populations grew. Because there was not always enough farmland to feed all the people, Greek city-states established colonies as far away as Sicily, North Africa, and the Black Sea.

The Delian League

During the 470s B.C. the Athenians created the Delian League. The league united several city-states and established a powerful navy to fight the Persian Empire. But the Athenians began to use the navy to expand their own empire. They forced the other league members to hand over territory, money, and ships. Athens continued to dominate the league, and the anger of the other members increased, eventually leading to the outbreak of the Peloponnesian Wars.

Trade between city-states and their new colonies enabled Greek merchants and craftspeople to prosper. These newly rich Greeks began to demand their share of power from the ruling nobles. In many city-states, merchants and artisans supported tyrants who seized power from the nobles. But when tyrants governed poorly, the people's resentment increased. In the city of Athens, rule by tyrants was replaced by democracy. Athenian citizens voted on many issues and elected their own leaders. Citizenship, however, was granted only to free men. Women and slaves, who made up a large part of Athens' population, could not be citizens.

Athens rose to a position of leadership among the Greek city-states. In the early 400s B.C., it led the resistance against the Persian invasions, winning great victories against larger armies and navies. After the victory over the Persians, Greece enjoyed a period known as the Golden Age. During the Golden Age, the Greek playwrights Aeschylus, Sophocles, and Euripides created dramas that explored human emotions and personalities. Socrates, a Greek PHILOSOPHER, taught his students to question their beliefs about every aspect of their lives, especially their beliefs about moral conduct. Greek scientists taught that natural events, such as illness, had natural causes and did not occur at the will of the gods.

During the Golden Age, Athens' power continued to grow, and other city-states, especially Sparta, became jealous. The rivalry between Athens and these other city-states led to the Peloponnesian Wars in the mid- to late 400s B.C. Sparta led a revolt against Athens, and Athens surrendered in 404 B.C. But some city-states resented Sparta's power just as much, so fighting continued for many years.

This statue, called the Victory of Samothrace, is one of the most famous works of Greek art. It portrays Athena Nike, the winged goddess of victory.

The Peloponnesian Wars had greatly weakened Greece. Around the same time, Macedonia, a region north of Greece, was becoming stronger. In the 330s B.C., Macedonian armies under King Philip II and his son, Alexander the Great, conquered Greece. The Macedonians admired the Greeks and adopted their culture. Philip II placed all of Greece under the power of his empire. Although it had been defeated, Greece was united for the first time in its long history.

By 146 B.C. the Romans had forced the Macedonians out of Greece and had seized control there. The Romans generally disliked the Greeks, but they respected Greek culture. They were influenced by the art, religion, and PHILOSOPHY of the Greeks and spread Greek culture throughout their vast empire. Greece in the A.D. 200s and 300s was dominated by invading Germanic peoples, who caused great suffering. From 400 on, Greece was part of the Eastern Roman Empire. The capital of this empire, Constantinople, was built on the site of a former Greek colony called Byzantium.

Gupta Dynasty

During the 200-year reign of the Gupta dynasty, ancient India enjoyed a golden age—a period of wealth, expansion, and advancement in the arts and sciences. The first Gupta emperor, Chandragupta I, founded the empire, which truly began to flourish under his son, Samudragupta, and his grandson, Chandragupta II. The empire spanned India from the Indus River in the west to the Brahmaputra River in the east, a distance of about 1,500 miles. Under the Gupta dynasty, Hinduism became the official religion. Scholars began to organize Hindu texts and teachings into the form that is still used today.

During this time, art, sculpture, music, dance, painting, and architecture flourished in an atmosphere of encouragement and admiration. Great scientific advances also occurred in India during this period. Physicians developed techniques for plastic surgery—surgery used to correct loss or injury of body parts. Indian chemists developed a way to keep certain metals from rusting.

Chandragupta II died around 414. Under the next few emperors, the Gupta dynasty slowly declined. In the mid-500s, India's influence was limited to the area around the eastern city of Bengal. (See also *Buddhism; Literature; Mathematics.*)

Helen of Troy

According to Greek legend, Helen of Troy was the most beautiful woman in the world. Every noble in Greece wanted to marry the beautiful Helen. She finally chose Menelaus, the king of the city-state of Sparta. Helen's sister, Clytemnestra, had already married Menelaus's brother, Agamemnon.

But Helen's beauty caused misfortune. During a visit to Sparta, a prince named Paris, from the city of Troy, fell in love with Helen. With the help of Aphrodite, the goddess of love, Paris won Helen's love and took her to Troy.

Menelaus was furious to find his queen gone. He and Agamemnon rallied many other Greek city-states against Troy. A huge Greek army surrounded Troy, and for the next ten years the Greeks and Trojans fought over Helen. In the end the Greeks destroyed the city, killed Paris, and returned Helen to Menelaus.

After Menelaus's death, Helen's stepsons forced her to leave Sparta. She went to the island of Rhodes, but her past caught up with her there. The husband of Polyxa, the queen of Rhodes, had been killed in the battle against the Trojans. Blaming Helen for her husband's death, Polyxa had her hanged. (See also *Homer; Trojan War.*)

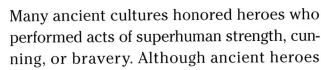
Heroes

Many ancient cultures honored heroes who performed acts of superhuman strength, cunning, or bravery. Although ancient heroes were usually human, some were the children of gods or goddesses. Ancient peoples celebrated their heroes with feasts and festivals.

Many heroes were considered demigods—beings who had more power than ordinary humans but less than a god. People often prayed to heroes for help when they did not want to disturb a god. In some cases a hero was believed to protect a particular city.

Heroes were especially important to the Greeks. The Greeks performed rituals and offered animal sacrifices at the burial places of their heroes. The most popular Greek hero was Heracles (also called Hercules), whose legendary strength enabled him to overpower kings, monsters, and even some gods.

Many other cultures included heroes in their myths. For example, the Chinese had legends about Yi the Excellent Archer. In one story, ten suns appeared in the sky, scorching the earth and destroying crops. With his magic bow and arrows, Yi shot down nine of the suns.

An EPIC from Mesopotamia tells the story of Gilgamesh, the ruler of a city-state called Uruk. Gilgamesh performed many brave acts, such as slaying a dragon and a gigantic bull. But in the end, he failed to win the prize he most wanted—a plant that would give him IMMORTALITY.

Many legends about heroes end with the hero's death. In some stories, however, the DEITIES ensured that the hero would continue to exist after death by making him or her into a part of nature, such as a constellation of stars. (See also *Gods and Goddesses; Homer.*)

One of the most popular heroes in both Greek and Roman mythology was Heracles. This Greek vase painting shows Heracles after he captured Cerberus, the ferocious three-headed dog that guarded the entrance to the underworld.

Hinduism

Hinduism is an ancient religion that developed in India and is still practiced there and throughout the world by millions of people. Its history began sometime after 2000 B.C., when people from central Asia—called Aryans—invaded India. The Aryan religion, based on sacred writings called the Vedas, spread throughout India and became the basis of Hinduism.

Some religious movements, such as Buddhism, challenged Hinduism around 500 B.C. In response, Hindu groups reorganized and renewed themselves, beginning the period of classical Hinduism that lasted until A.D. 1000. During that time, most of the basic literature, beliefs, and practices of Hinduism were established.

The followers of Hinduism worship the gods Brahma (the supreme god), Vishnu (god of protection), and Shiva (god of creation and destruction) as well as several others. According to Hindu belief, gods and goddesses have many human traits and often interact with humans on earth. Hindus worship at shrines, in temples, and at home. They also consider many aspects of nature to be sacred, including rivers and animals.

Hinduism organizes people into castes, or *jāti*—an Indian term that means "group by birth." There are five main castes: priests; rulers and warriors; merchants and professionals; laborers and servants; and untouchables, who perform the jobs that are considered too lowly for the other classes.

Hinduism is concerned with social behavior as much as with worship. Therefore, members of each caste must live up to the duties of the group, or dharma. Hindus believe that the soul is reborn many times in new bodies. The behavior of an individual, or karma, determines where he or she will go in the next life.

Hinduism has several sacred texts, which explain and reflect all aspects of Hindu life and belief. The Code of Manu, produced between 200 B.C. and A.D. 200, outlines laws and duties. In the Bhagavad Gita, the prince Arjuna receives religious guidance from Vishnu, who is disguised as Arjuna's chariot driver Krishna. (See also *Christianity; Gods and Goddesses; Judaism; Myths and Legends.*)

Shiva, the Hindu god of justice, time, creation, and destruction, is shown here with his wife, Parvati. They are enthroned on a white bull called Nandi.

54

History

History is the story of the past. Sometimes history tries to explain past events; at other times it simply records them. The earliest civilizations passed their history from generation to generation orally—in the form of stories and legends.

As written language developed, history became a type of record keeping. In ancient Egypt, around 2600 B.C., priests and other high officials wrote accounts of the lives of their rulers. Such histories usually presented only a positive portrait of the ruler and said little about the everyday lives of the people.

Chinese historians began keeping historical records as early as 1000 B.C. Working in the courts of emperors, they came to appreciate the vast scope of history, including politics, economics, morality, social life, and nature. They also tried to learn from history by judging the skills of past rulers. One of the greatest Chinese historians was Sima Qian, who lived around 100 B.C. His *Records of the Historians* covered 2,000 years in 130 chapters, most of which are biographies of famous people.

The Maya recorded the important events in the lives of their rulers on stelae—stones with carved images. The Maya stela shown here is located in present-day Honduras.

The Greeks developed their own historical tradition. Greek historians considered their work a form of literature. Their main goal was to give accurate information—in a fine literary style—and to offer judgments about their subjects.

Herodotus, who wrote in the 400s B.C., is often called the father of history. In his *Histories,* he focused on the long rivalry between the Greeks and the Persians. He crafted a story with a MORAL theme—that evil will be punished, but good people may not always have good fortune. Polybius, a later Greek historian, traveled to important battle sites to gather information from eyewitnesses.

Roman historians often included their opinions in their works. Tacitus, who wrote about the history of the Roman Empire, expressed his dislike for some past emperors. As Christianity spread throughout the Roman Empire, historians recognized that the Old Testament had been one of the earliest models of historical writing.

Homer

The Greek poet Homer is considered the first great ancient poet. His EPICS, the *Iliad* and the *Odyssey,* influenced the history and culture of ancient Greece. Very little is known about his life, except that he probably lived during the 800s or 700s B.C. His poems are written in the version of Greek spoken in Ionia, a settlement on the west coast of Asia Minor. Because of this, it is believed that he came from that region. According to legend, Homer was blind.

Historians believe that Homer wrote the *Iliad* first. The *Iliad* tells of events that occurred during the Trojan War, which was fought between Greece and the city of Troy. In the story, the Greek hero Achilles becomes angry and refuses to help his fellow Greeks fight the Trojans. But when his closest friend, Patroclus, is killed by the Trojan hero Hector, Achilles returns to battle and kills Hector for revenge. Achilles shows compassion by returning Hector's body to the dead man's grieving father, King Priam.

The *Odyssey* reveals a lighter side of Homer's poetry. It follows the Greek hero Odysseus and his companions as they make their way home after the Trojan War. Odysseus endures ten years of dangerous encounters. He meets fantastic creatures, such as singing mermaids called Sirens and a one-eyed giant, Polyphemus the Cyclops. At last he returns home to his wife, Penelope, and chases away the men who want to marry her.

Greek poetry of Homer's time was intended to be recited or sung before an audience. Poets, or bards, were storytellers who created legends that were told and retold for generations. When people eventually wrote down Homer's poems, they probably only came close to his actual words. He often repeated certain words and phrases, which helped him and his audience to remember the poems.

Even so, Homer's use of language was not simple or commonplace. He was a master of the sound of language, using smooth, flowing words to describe peaceful scenes, or sharp, short words to convey anger and battle. He was also skillful at building suspense by hinting at events that would occur later in his stories. His works were studied for centuries by ancient Greeks and Romans, and they are still read and enjoyed by both children and adults. (See also *Helen of Troy; Literature.*)

This painted vase illustrates a famous story from the Odyssey. *It shows Odysseus, the story's hero, and his men using a sharpened, red-hot stick to blind Polyphemus, the one-eyed monster who had eaten many of Odysseus's men.*

Jerusalem

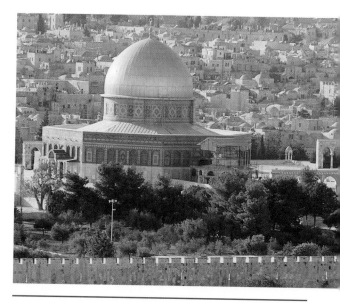

Jerusalem is sacred to three major world religions—Judaism, Christianity, and Islam. In the foreground of this photograph are the walls of the old city, which was built by the Jews. Behind them is the Dome of the Rock, sacred to the Muslims. In the distance (but not shown) is the Mount of Olives, where Jesus prayed before his crucifixion.

The first people to settle in Jerusalem were the Canaanites, around 2500 B.C. Located along a high mountain pass used by traveling merchants, the city gradually grew in importance.

In about 1000 B.C., Jerusalem was conquered by King David, ruler of the Jewish people. David made Jerusalem his capital. The city flourished under the rule of David's son, King Solomon, who built the Temple—Judaism's most sacred building.

Jerusalem was independent until 587 B.C., when the Babylonian emperor Nebuchadnezzar II conquered the city and destroyed the Temple. The emperor forced the Jews to move to Babylonia. Fifty years later, the Persians conquered the Babylonians and permitted the Jews to return to Jerusalem and rebuild their temple.

The Jews continued to live under the rule of powerful foreign rulers. In the 160s B.C., the Seleucids tried to force the Jews to worship Greek gods. In response, a family of Jewish priests called the Maccabees led a rebellion and reestablished Jewish independence.

The Jews ruled themselves for about 100 years, until the Roman general Pompey conquered the region (then called Judaea) in 63 B.C. The Romans later chose a Jew, King Herod I, to rule Judaea. Herod rebuilt Jerusalem and the Temple, but the Jews continued to resist Roman rule. In order to strengthen their power over the Jews, the Romans made Judaea an official PROVINCE of their empire. As Roman rule became more harsh, dissatisfaction grew among the Jews.

The Jews seized control of Jerusalem in A.D. 66, during a rebellion known as the Jewish War. Four years later, Roman troops captured Jerusalem and destroyed the Temple in bloody fighting. Despite the common belief that it was impossible to defeat the armies of Rome, the Jews rebelled again in 132. The rebels were crushed, and this time the Romans forbade Jews to live in Jerusalem. Many Jews scattered throughout Europe, Arabia, and North Africa.

Jesus

Jesus was a Jewish teacher whose followers founded the Christian religion. Most information about him comes from the Gospels, accounts of his life written by the Apostles Matthew, Mark, Luke, and John—4 of his 12 closest students.

Jesus' Hebrew name was Yeshua (Joshua). He was born just before the beginning of the current era, which is referred to as A.D. The abbreviation A.D. stands for *anno Domini* ("in the year of the Lord") and refers to dates since the birth of Jesus. Jesus was born in Bethlehem in Judaea (present-day Israel) to a woman named Mary who was married to Joseph, a carpenter. Before Mary's child was born, the angel Gabriel told her that she would have a special child. Christians believe that Jesus was the Son of God.

In about A.D. 29, Jesus encountered a Jewish PROPHET, whom he named John the Baptist. According to the Gospels, John recognized that Jesus was the Messiah—the leader who would bring the Kingdom of God to earth.

Jesus began to preach in public. He reached out to the lowest classes of society, such as the poor and the sick. Many of those who heard him were Jews, but he also invited non-Jews to follow him. According to the Gospels, he performed miracles, such as turning water into wine and healing sick people. He also criticized some Jewish customs and Roman laws.

This mosaic shows Jesus symbolically giving the keys to the kingdom of heaven to St. Peter, one of his most trusted disciples.

As Jesus' reputation spread, the Roman government and Jewish religious leaders began to oppose him. Both groups feared that he would weaken their power. They were also angered by his claims that human kingdoms and laws would be replaced by the Kingdom of God.

In about A.D. 30, Jesus was arrested and sentenced to die for blasphemy—the act of insulting something considered to be sacred. Jesus' followers despaired, but he had taught them that suffering is part of one's devotion to God. He said he would suffer so that God would forgive their sins. The Romans crucified him—nailing his hands and feet to a large wooden cross and leaving him to die.

His followers buried his body, and the Gospels recount the story that three days later, the tomb was empty. The Apostles had visions of him and told the other followers that Jesus had risen from the dead and was in heaven. Jesus came to be known as the Christ, meaning "savior" in Greek. Many new followers joined the Apostles, and in time their beliefs developed into a religion that is now called Christianity.

Judaism

Judaism is the religion of the Jewish people. According to Jewish tradition, the first Jew was Abraham, a shepherd who came to Canaan (present-day Israel) sometime after 2000 B.C. His DESCENDANTS were slaves in Egypt until a PROPHET named Moses led them back to Canaan.

Unlike many other ancient peoples, the Jews worshiped only one god. They believed that God had promised to protect them as his chosen people. In return, the Jews promised to obey God's laws. However, Jews sometimes worshiped the gods of their PAGAN neighbors. Prophets came forth to remind Jews of their promise to obey and worship only God. Then, in the 500s B.C., the Babylonians conquered the Jews, destroyed their temple in Jerusalem, and forced them into slavery in Babylonia (present-day Iraq). After this catastrophe, Jewish leaders made greater efforts to preserve Judaism.

The history of the Jewish people had been passed down over the centuries mainly in spoken form. Some Jews had written down religious teachings, such as traditional prayers and the speeches of their prophets. By the 400s B.C., five books of sacred writings, called the Torah, had been written. These writings form the first five books of the Bible. The Torah, which includes the Ten Commandments, explains how to live a daily life of justice, humility, charity, and devotion.

In A.D. 66, the Jews revolted against Roman rule. Four years later, the Romans defeated the rebels and destroyed the Second Temple, which had been built after the Jews returned to their homeland from Babylonia. However, the western wall of the Second Temple remained standing. This wall became known as the Wailing Wall, and today it is considered the most sacred place of prayer for Jews.

The Diaspora

In A.D. 132, the Jews attempted to overthrow their Roman rulers. The Romans defeated the rebels three years later and forbade Jews to visit or live in Jerusalem, Judaism's most sacred city. Because of this, Jews were scattered through Europe, Arabia, and North Africa. This resettlement of the Jewish people throughout the ancient world is known as the Diaspora, from Greek words meaning "to disperse or scatter."

In A.D. 70, Rome crushed a Jewish rebellion in Jerusalem. This sculpture is from the Arch of Titus—a monument commemorating Rome's victory over the rebels. It shows triumphant Roman soldiers stealing Jerusalem's treasures, including a large menorah.

The first five Roman emperors—Augustus and the four emperors who followed him—are known as the Julio-Claudian emperors. They ruled Rome from 27 B.C. to A.D. 68—almost 100 years. The second emperor, Tiberius, was the stepson of Augustus. Although he was unpopular, Tiberius was an able ruler who continued many of the policies of Augustus. Eventually his long rule sank into suspicion and violence as he began to order the execution of some of his own advisers and relatives. Many Romans celebrated when he died.

Conditions grew even worse under the third emperor, Gaius Caesar Germanicus, who took power in A.D. 37. When he was a child, his mother dressed him in a full military uniform, for which he was nicknamed Caligula, meaning "baby boots." Caligula showed great promise when he became emperor at age 25. But he soon fell ill, and when he recovered, he was greatly changed. He killed enemies and friends alike, and his cruel nature often shocked and horrified people.

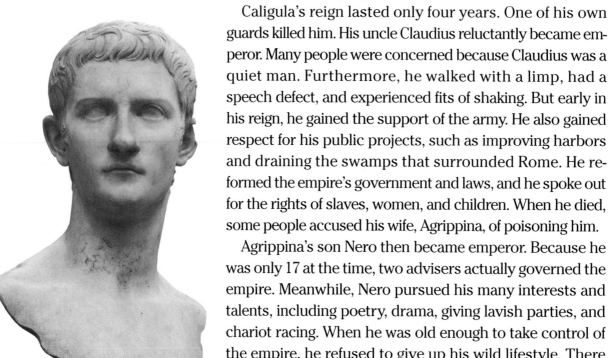

Caligula was perhaps the most hated Roman emperor. Once, at a banquet, he laughed aloud and told his guests that he could have their throats cut right there.

Caligula's reign lasted only four years. One of his own guards killed him. His uncle Claudius reluctantly became emperor. Many people were concerned because Claudius was a quiet man. Furthermore, he walked with a limp, had a speech defect, and experienced fits of shaking. But early in his reign, he gained the support of the army. He also gained respect for his public projects, such as improving harbors and draining the swamps that surrounded Rome. He reformed the empire's government and laws, and he spoke out for the rights of slaves, women, and children. When he died, some people accused his wife, Agrippina, of poisoning him.

Agrippina's son Nero then became emperor. Because he was only 17 at the time, two advisers actually governed the empire. Meanwhile, Nero pursued his many interests and talents, including poetry, drama, giving lavish parties, and chariot racing. When he was old enough to take control of the empire, he refused to give up his wild lifestyle. There was a great fire in Rome during his reign, and legend says that carefree Nero played his fiddle as the city burned. He blamed the Christians for starting the fire and persecuted them. As his hold on power weakened, he began to suspect that plots were being hatched against him. He ordered the deaths of many people, including his mother and his wife. When the army finally rebelled, Nero left the city and killed himself. (See also *Antonine Emperors*.)

Law

Laws are rules that govern the behavior of people in a society. Laws identify what is or is not allowed and how people will be punished for crimes. In most early societies, laws were based on local traditions and customs as well as on the decisions of community leaders. Because these laws were not written down, they have been lost to history. When people began to write down their laws, the laws became separated from the rulers who had created them. The laws remained while rulers rose and fell.

One of the first organized systems of law appeared around 4000 B.C. in ancient Egypt. The kings issued the laws. In the royal palaces, judges held court and heard cases brought by the people.

In the 1700s B.C., the Babylonian king Hammurabi ordered that his laws be carved into a stela—a large, carved stone pillar. The Code of Hammurabi, one of the first known written sets of laws, was organized into several areas, including family, business, and property. Hammurabi's code aimed to protect ordinary citizens from abuse by more powerful people, and it provided severe punishments for crimes. Many of its laws are similar to modern ones. For example, ancient Babylonians who spoke in court had to swear to tell the truth.

Religion played a role in many ancient law codes, governing relations between DEITIES and humans as well as among people. Many ancient civilizations, including the Egyptians, Babylonians, and Jews, believed that their laws were given to them by their gods.

Around 200 B.C., Hindu priests collected Indian laws into a work called the Code of Manu. This code defines the specific duties and responsibilities of the individual within his or her caste, or social class. Hindu society, like most ancient societies, imposed different laws on different classes.

One of the most important ancient law codes belonged to the Romans. They first wrote down their laws in about 450 B.C. Known as the Twelve Tables, these laws were carved in stone and displayed in public. Over time, the Romans produced a huge set of detailed laws, which they brought to all the regions they ruled. Roman law became the foundation for modern laws in Europe and elsewhere. (See also *Democracy; Hinduism; Judaism; Rome.*)

At the top of this stela, or stone pillar, Hammurabi receives the laws from the sun god Shamash. Beneath them are the laws, engraved in an ancient form of writing called cuneiform.

Literature

The earliest works of literature consisted of words that were valued for their power, beauty, and meaning. Because most ancient peoples could neither read nor write, most of these early works were spoken or sung. As people developed alphabets and other forms of writing, works were written down. Ancient literature included stories, poems, histories, letters, speeches, and plays. These works expressed the customs, beliefs, and values of the people who created them. Today they are read for pleasure as well as to learn about the lives of ancient people.

Some ancient stories expressed peoples' ideas about history. These stories became sacred myths, legends, and histories. For example, the *Enuma Elish,* a collection of Babylonian myths, tells a story of the creation of the world. According to this legend, there was a battle among the gods. When the battle was over, the world was created from the body of a god who had been killed during the fighting. Then the gods created humans to serve them as slaves. Similarly, stories from the history of the Greeks were retold by the poet Homer in the *Iliad* and the *Odyssey* and by the poet Hesiod in *Theogony*—all three composed around 800 B.C.

Most of these early works were long poems called EPICS, composed and recited aloud for an audience. The musical quality of the language and rhythm of the verse helped both the poet and the audience to remember the poems. The poets also repeated many phrases. Homer, for example, often repeated the phrase "the grey-eyed goddess" when speaking of the goddess Athena.

Scratching the Surface

The literature of ancient times was written on several different materials. Around 3100 B.C., the Sumerians developed a system of pressing characters into clay tablets. Around 2500 B.C., the Egyptians invented papyrus—fragile, paperlike sheets made from the soft sponge inside marsh reeds. Most Egyptian texts were rolled into scrolls. Paper was invented by the Chinese around A.D. 100, but they kept their method of making paper a secret for more than 500 years.

As societies developed or adopted alphabets and systems of writing, they recorded these poems and stories permanently. One of the first known works of literature to be written down was the Book of the Dead, in which the Egyptians described the afterlife. The book contains many prayers and spells that were supposed to guide a soul through death and protect it from evil.

Since memorizing was no longer necessary, writers could produce instruction manuals, histories, and books on such subjects as PHILOSOPHY, geography, and mathematics. The great Roman statesman and military leader Julius Caesar wrote *Gallic War.* Considered to be one of the finest examples of ancient PROSE, *Gallic War* describes Caesar's conquest of Gaul (present-day France). The book is still studied for its detailed accounts of battles and its skillful use of the Latin language.

As the knowledge of writing spread, more poets and writers began to address everyday subjects, such as their own feelings. Augustine, a Catholic bishop in North Africa, wrote his *Confessions,* considered to be the first true autobiography. Born a PAGAN, Augustine tells the story of his childhood and the events that led him to convert to Christianity.

Literature flourished, but written texts were extremely rare, fragile, and precious. Societies built libraries to hold their collections. In the 600s B.C., the Assyrian king Ashurbanipal built a library in the city of Nineveh. The library contained thousands of clay tablets with laws, poems, and the records of astronomers, merchants, and the royal court. The most famous library of the ancient world was at Alexandria in Egypt. Rulers ordered SCRIBES to make copies of any book that passed through the region. When the library was destroyed by a fire around 47 B.C., hundreds of thousands of ancient works were lost.

Although writers and written works were increasing in number, literacy—the ability to read and write—remained out of the reach of

The Epic of Gilgamesh, *written in Mesopotamia about 4,000 years ago, is one of the world's oldest surviving works of literature. This sculpture shows King Gilgamesh taming a lion with his bare hands.*

most people. In most ancient societies, literacy was limited to priests, high government officials, and scribes. In fact, most people never saw a written document during their lifetimes. This situation changed somewhat during Greek and Roman times, when such skills were available to anyone who could afford an education—still less than half the population. (See also *Art; Drama; History; Muses; Oratory; Philosophy; Poetry; Schools.*)

The Maccabees were a family of Jewish priests in Judaea (a region of ancient Palestine) who led a rebellion to save their religion. In the 100s B.C., Palestine was ruled by the Seleucid DYNASTY, which also ruled Asia Minor, part of Egypt, and Syria. Antiochus IV, the Seleucid king, used the Syrian army to try to strengthen his power in Palestine by destroying Judaism. He forbade Jews to practice their religion and forced them to worship Greek gods.

The rebellion began around 168 B.C. near the city of Jerusalem, where the Syrians had set up an altar to the Greek god Zeus. When a Jewish man approached the altar to make a sacrifice to Zeus, a Jewish priest named Mattathias stepped forward in rage and killed the man, whom he regarded as disloyal. He then issued a call for Jews to gather in the hills around the city.

Mattathias died soon after, and one of his five sons—Judah— took command of the rebel army. His forces grew when a group of strict, religious Jews who normally kept to themselves joined the rebellion. With daring and luck, the vastly outnumbered Jews won a series of victories against the Syrian armies. Judah earned the name of Maccabeus ("the Hammer").

The rebels' greatest victory came in 164 B.C., when they reclaimed the Temple in Jerusalem, removed the Greek altars and idols, and rededicated it to God. This event is still celebrated in the Jewish holiday of Hanukkah.

When Antiochus died the following year, some of the rebels felt that they had achieved their goal of preserving Judaism, and they withdrew from the fighting. The war continued, however, and Judah fell in battle in 161 B.C. His brothers, Jonathan and Simon, continued to lead the struggle and succeeded in capturing much of Palestine.

In 139 B.C. Palestine became an independent Jewish nation. The Maccabee family ruled the Jews as kings and priests for about 80 years, until the Romans themselves conquered Judaea in 63 B.C.

After the Maccabees recaptured their temple from the Romans, they lit a menorah, a seven-branched candlestick like the one shown here. According to legend, a one-day supply of oil kept the light burning for eight days.

64

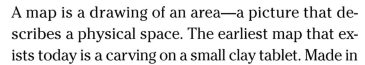

Maps

A map is a drawing of an area—a picture that describes a physical space. The earliest map that exists today is a carving on a small clay tablet. Made in Mesopotamia around 2500 B.C., it shows the property of an ancient landowner. In the 1300s B.C., the Egyptians began to use maps to show property boundaries for purposes of taxation. This was necessary because the Nile River flooded its banks and washed away the markers that the people had set up on their land.

The ancient Greeks, who traded in the Mediterranean region and colonized much of that area, used the knowledge they gained to make maps that accurately depicted the size and shape of their world. In the 500s B.C., the Greek PHILOSOPHER Anaximander made the first map of the entire known world. Two other Greeks—Eratosthenes (a mathematician) and Hipparchus (an astronomer)—developed the system of horizontal and vertical lines that are now called lines of latitude and longitude.

In the A.D. 100s, the Greek geographer and mathematician Ptolemy produced an eight-volume work called *Geography*. This very important work contained maps that covered the region from Scotland to central Africa. Although Ptolemy's maps contained many errors, they were used by other mapmakers for many centuries.

The Romans learned their mapmaking skills from the Greeks. Focusing on military conquest and control of their empire, Roman mapmakers took special note of roads, bridges, and other such features. Maps showing property boundaries were displayed in the central open area of each city.

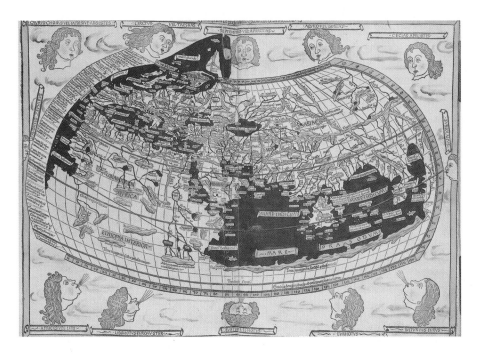

This map, created in the A.D. 100s, is based on the descriptions of Ptolemy in his eight-volume work called Geography.

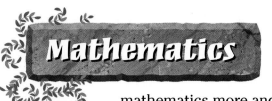
Mathematics

The earliest form of mathematics—the science of numbers—was simple counting. As people developed agriculture, trade, and cities, they needed mathematics more and more. From the number of seeds to the number of citizens, mathematics became an important part of everyday life.

Many ancient mathematicians were also priests. They studied the sun, moon, stars, and planets and made calculations about the passage of time. Then they recommended the best times to plant seeds, harvest crops, or celebrate religious holidays and festivals.

Much of ancient mathematics was arithmetic—addition, subtraction, multiplication, and division. But ancient peoples also understood geometry—the branch of mathematics that deals with angles, areas, shapes, and space. The first peoples to develop an understanding of mathematics were the Egyptians and the Babylonians.

The Egyptians created a counting system based on the number 10. Around 1700 B.C., the Babylonians developed their own system, based on groups of 60. Both systems are still in use—ten dimes in a dollar, 60 minutes in an hour. By about 1500 B.C., both civilizations were probably using fractions to indicate parts of a whole.

Many ancient civilizations, including the Greeks and Romans, used an abacus to perform simple calculations. An abacus is a device that consists of columns of beads strung on wires or rods that are attached to the inside edges of a frame. Beads are moved from one side of the frame to the other to perform simple calculations.

In ancient Greece, mathematics was studied as part of PHILOSOPHY, not just as a method of solving everyday problems. In the 500s B.C., the Greek philosopher-mathematicians Thales and Pythagoras are believed to have introduced geometry—the study of shapes. Since they left no writings, however, historians are uncertain as to what they actually knew about geometry. Around 300 B.C. another Greek mathematician, Euclid, summarized what was known about mathematics in his book *Elements of Geometry*. Euclid emphasized the use of a logical sequence of steps to prove that a statement is true. Each step of the proof is based on a previously proven step. Euclid's method, known as deductive reasoning, was a key element of Greek philosophy and politics.

Greek geometry reached its peak in the A.D. 100s with the astronomer and geographer Ptolemy. His knowledge and skill led him to propose that the earth

Zeno's Paradoxes

Zeno, a Greek philosopher of the 400s B.C., showed how logic can sometimes lead to false or ridiculous conclusions. He created paradoxes—ideas that seem to be true but are actually false. He proposed that an arrow shot from a bow would never reach its target. Why? Because the arrow must first travel half the distance toward its target, then half the remaining distance, then half again, and so on. The arrow will approach, but it can never strike. A real arrow, of course, will cover the entire distance.

Archimedes was one of the greatest mathematicians of ancient Greece. The story of his death shows his powers of concentration. He was so absorbed in a mathematical problem that he failed to notice a battle raging around him. He was killed by a Roman soldier, as shown in this mosaic.

was the center of the universe and that the sun, moon, and stars revolved around it. Using mathematics, another Greek astronomer, Eratosthenes, accurately calculated the distance around the earth.

The Romans' most lasting contribution to mathematics was Roman numerals, which are still used (though only in special circumstances). Roman numerals are combinations of seven symbols: I, V, X, L, C, D, and M. These represent the numbers 1, 5, 10, 50, 100, 500, and 1,000. When the symbol for a smaller number is placed *after* a symbol for a bigger number, you add the two. Thus, VI is V plus I, or 6. When a symbol for a smaller number is placed *before* a larger number, you subtract the two. Thus, IV is V minus I, or 4. The numbers 1, 2, 3, 4, and 5 would be written in Roman numerals as I, II, III, IV, and V. The number 210 is written as CCX, and 40 is written as XL. Roman numerals worked well for small numbers but not for larger numbers.

Around 200 B.C., the idea of negative numbers emerged in China, and later in India. Negative numbers were used at first to represent debts, or money that was owed. The Mayan people of Mexico and Central America invented the concept of zero in the A.D. 300s. Zero was invented independently by Indian mathematicians about 500 years later. By the late 1400s, the idea of zero had spread from India to Europe and had become the basis for the system of Arabic numerals. Today this system, composed of the ten digits 0, 1, 2, 3, 4, 5, 6, 7, 8, and 9, is used nearly worldwide. (See also *Calendars; Science and Technology.*)

Maya

The ancient Maya built a great civilization in the rain forests, high plains, volcanic mountains, and valleys of southeastern Mexico and northern Central America. Dozens of tribes lived in Mexico and Central America for thousands of years before the Olmec people formed the region's first advanced society, around 1200 B.C. About 200 years later, the Maya began to adopt Olmec religious practices and artistic styles, and they gradually rose to prominence in the region.

By the time the Olmec civilization disappeared, around 400 B.C., the Maya had developed advanced agricultural systems that helped them establish permanent settlements and increase their population. They moved from small villages into larger cities, and a small ruling class of nobles and priests emerged. Mayan cities contained large ceremonial buildings with elaborate carvings and sculptures of their rulers, gods, and goddesses. In fact, some Mayan rulers were shown as gods, suggesting that they ruled by DIVINE authority.

The Maya worshiped many gods. The most important Mayan DEITIES included Chac (the rain god), Itzamna (the sky god), and Kukulcan (the creator god). Religion influenced all aspects of Mayan life: birth, coming of age, choosing one's heir, waging war, and death. The Maya believed that when nobles died, they became gods. Sometimes they constructed pyramids over the tombs of their dead kings to serve as shrines. People also worshiped their dead relatives and buried them beneath the family home.

Ball Game

The Maya played a ball game as part of a religious ceremony. Two teams of players competed to keep a hard rubber ball—representing the world—in the air, using only their knees, buttocks, and hips. The game ended if the ball passed through one of the small stone hoops on the side walls of the ball court. Some historians believe that the players were often slaves or prisoners. They were freed if they won, or sacrificed to the gods if they lost.

Blood was also important in Mayan religion and culture. It symbolized life and death, and the Maya drew it from their own bodies as well as from the bodies of the slaves and prisoners they captured during their frequent conflicts with neighboring tribes. In fact, the Maya often sacrificed these captives as offerings to their gods because they believed that human sacrifice was necessary to maintain the stability of the world. Other victims included ordinary citizens who failed to obey the priests. Sometimes the Maya sought to purchase the favors of their gods with offerings of human blood.

There was no single Mayan language but several different languages that were spoken in different Mayan cities. Some of the Mayan languages are Quiche, Cakchiquel, Tzeltal, Chontal, and Tzotzil. Many of these languages are still spoken in parts of Mexico,

Guatemala, and Belize. The Maya learned to write from other tribes, possibly the Zapotecs. They recorded their myths and rituals on stone slabs or pillars, called stelae. They also wrote codices—books made from the fibers of the maguey plant. The most important Mayan work is the *Popol Vuh,* a CHRONICLE of the Maya and their kings and heroes.

The Maya were the first people in the Americas to keep historical records. These involved detailed ASTRONOMICAL calendars that associated

This mural is from Bonampak, an ancient Mayan site in southern Mexico. The painting shows musicians marching in a religious ceremony.

dates with events in the lives of important people and gods. They were called ritual calendars or the divinatory calendars, and they consisted of 364 days divided into 28 months of 13 days each.

From A.D. 250 to 550, the Maya also had much contact with the people of Teotihuacán, a city-state in central Mexico. Through this interaction the Maya adopted many new gods and new styles of art and clothing. By 550 the Mayan kingdom had grown to include several noble families. They also had many well-established cities and city-states. Up to 100,000 people may have lived in the largest city, Tikal (in present-day Guatemala). Mayan astronomers built large observatories to study the skies. They used advanced mathematics to study the movements of heavenly bodies. The Maya also built several palaces, temples, and other structures, the ruins of which are found in Palenque, Uxmal, Copán, and Chichén Itzá. These structures were usually large pyramids made of earth and stone. Mayan homes were generally built with sun-dried clay and palms.

The Maya civilization flourished until about 900, when wars and FAMINE weakened the once powerful city-states and noble families. The Maya and their culture lived on, but other peoples, particularly the Aztecs, came to dominate the region.

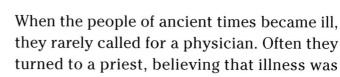

Medicine

When the people of ancient times became ill, they rarely called for a physician. Often they turned to a priest, believing that illness was caused by gods, demons, or spirits. Treatments generally included sacrifices, magical spells, and religious rituals. Priests, or shamans, often knew something about healing, combining magic with herbs, potions, and other remedies.

Such treatments are commonly known today as folk medicine. Folk healers knew about many plants and animal products that relieved pain and cured certain illnesses. For example, some ancient healers used willow bark to relieve pain. Today, scientists know that willow bark contains a substance similar to a chemical found in aspirin. Many healers also knew how to set broken bones and perform other medical procedures.

Some healers became professional physicians and spent their lives treating wealthy patients, training students, and writing books. One of the first such doctors was Imhotep, who lived in Egypt around 2800 B.C. Egyptian physicians learned to look for signs of illness and to suggest treatments that had worked in the past.

The law code of the Babylonian king Hammurabi included a list of illnesses that a healer could treat and specified the amount of money he was permitted to charge. Written in the 1700s B.C., the code also listed punishments for any harm done to a patient.

India's first great physician, Charaka, lived around 1000 B.C. His teachings formed the basis of *Ayurveda,* an organized system of medicine that emphasized the prevention of illness. It also stressed the idea of balance among the body's substances, including bone, MARROW, blood, fat, MUCUS, and air. Ayurvedic physicians knew little about ANATOMY because the Hindu religion forbade dissection—the cutting of dead bodies for study. Even so, Ayurvedic books describe more than 100 different tools for surgery, and Indian physicians successfully performed many kinds of operations, including amputations.

In neighboring China, physicians focused on the body's balance of yin and yang, the two basic forces in the universe. Yin and yang supposedly

The God of Healing

Asclepius was the Greek god of healing. People visited his many temples throughout Greece, often sleeping inside them overnight. They believed that Asclepius would appear in their dreams and tell them how to cure their illnesses. They showed their appreciation by leaving behind models of body parts made of stone and clay.

Roman physicians were skilled at performing minor surgery. This painting shows a Roman doctor using a surgical tool to remove an arrow from a wounded soldier's leg.

flow through 12 invisible channels in the body, which physicians monitored by checking 51 different pulses. Chinese physicians still use acupuncture, the practice of inserting long needles into the channels to control the balance of yin and yang. By 300 B.C., Chinese physicians, such as Hua To, also knew how to use ANESTHESIA and to perform surgery on living patients.

In ancient Greece, the earliest medical practices included religious rituals and worship at temples. But some healers turned to a more scientific approach. They hoped that by learning how a healthy body works, they could understand how to heal a diseased one. Hippocrates, who lived in the 400s B.C., taught his students about diet, anatomy, surgery, and medications. He also established the Hippocratic Oath, which requires physicians to swear that they will do only what is good for the patient. Physicians still take this ancient oath before beginning to practice medicine.

Like Hinduism, Greek religion disapproved of dissection. But two Greek doctors—Herophilus and Erasistratus—ignored this rule and learned much about anatomy by studying the organs of dead people. Galen, a Greek living in Rome in the A.D. 100s, dissected apes and compared their bodies to human ones. He also developed the theory that four fluids—blood, mucus, black bile, and yellow bile—must be balanced within the body in order to maintain good health. Galen served as physician to a Roman emperor, and his theories—even those that were wrong—formed the basis of European medicine for many centuries. (See also *Science and Technology.*)

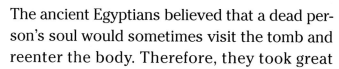

Mummies

The ancient Egyptians believed that a dead person's soul would sometimes visit the tomb and reenter the body. Therefore, they took great care to preserve dead bodies. During the earliest centuries of Egyptian civilization, before 3000 B.C., Egyptians did little to prepare dead bodies for burial. They wrapped the corpses in mats of plant fibers and buried them in sandy, shallow graves. Since bodies quickly dried out in the region's desert climate, they decayed very little.

Later the Egyptians buried their dead in wooden coffins, deep in underground tombs. These tombs had large stone rooms in which the coffins were placed. Such burials protected the bodies from weather, robbers, and wild animals. But in the damp, closed tombs, bodies decayed quickly.

To preserve the bodies of important people, Egyptians developed elaborate procedures for embalming, or preserving, the bodies. A surgeon made a cut on the left side and removed all the internal organs, except the heart. After soaking the entire body in a salt solution called natron, he refilled the midsection with a mixture of spices and plant gums.

The next step involved wrapping the body carefully in many layers of linen and other cloths, with religious objects placed between the layers. Sometimes a layer of plaster was applied to the wrapped body, or mummy. Artists painted facial features and other decorations on the plaster after it dried and hardened. Finally, the body was placed inside a wooden coffin. Some coffins were decorated with elaborate carvings and artwork, depending on the wealth and importance of the dead person.

Detailed instructions for embalming appear in the Book of the Dead, a guide for ancient Egyptian embalmers. The Greek historian Herodotus and the Book of Genesis in the Bible refer to the Egyptian practice of embalming.

In modern times, mummies were prized by robbers, collectors, historians, and museums. Scientists have learned much about ancient Egyptian culture, religion, health, and diet by examining mummified bodies. (See also *Archaeology; Myths and Legends; Underworld.*)

The mummified bodies of wealthy and important ancient Egyptians were placed in elaborately decorated coffins. This photograph shows a coffin that has been painted with scenes from the life of the dead person.

Muses

The Muses were the ancient Greek goddesses of the arts. At first, there were three: Melete (goddess of practice), Mneme (goddess of memory), and Aoede (goddess of song). Then, in the 700s B.C., the Greek poet Hesiod wrote the *Theogony,* a long poem in which he listed nine Muses to rule over the arts.

The roles and duties of the Muses changed slightly over time, particularly when the Romans adopted them into their worship. The nine Muses and their usual areas of responsibility are Calliope (epic poetry), Clio (history), Erato (LYRIC poetry and songs), Euterpe (flute playing), Melpomene (tragedy), Polyhymnia (HYMNS and PANTOMIME), Terpsichore (choral poetry and dance), Thalia (comedy), and Urania (astronomy).

The origin of the Muses reflects Greek ideas about the nature of art and creativity. Their father was Zeus, the supreme god and god of lightning. Their mother was Mnemosyne, the goddess of memory. Although the Muses were

This mosaic shows two Muses standing beside the Roman poet Virgil. The Muse holding the scroll of paper is Clio, goddess of history. The Muse holding the mask is Melpomene, goddess of tragedy.

not among the most powerful gods, they lived on Mount Olympus with the others. They were guided by Apollo, the god of music, prophecy, and light.

When not on Mount Olympus, the Muses favored a sacred fountain on Mount Helicon. The Greeks believed that anyone who drank from this fountain would receive the power of artistic creativity. This myth relates to one of the Muses' most important roles—inspiring artists.

Hesiod, Homer, and many other poets addressed their poems to the Muses, calling on them for inspiration. The Greek PHILOSOPHER Plato wrote that artists were "possessed" by the Muses in a kind of "divine madness." However, Plato distrusted such unpredictable power. Despite Plato's opposition, the Muses remained vital and popular figures in both Greek and Roman mythology. Artists often depicted them in MOSAICS, paintings, and sculptures. Their name is the origin of the word *museum,* which once meant "a place of the Muses," and *music,* which meant "art of the Muses."

In ancient societies, music and dance had deep religious meaning. Music and dance brought people together in social activities. In this way, music and dance became art forms presented for the enjoyment of audiences.

ARCHAEOLOGISTS have found musical instruments that were made nearly 30,000 years ago. Most early musical devices were percussion instruments, which were struck to produce a rhythmic beat or a tone. Drums and rattles were among the most common percussion instruments. In religious rituals and celebrations, musicians beat rhythms while dancers stamped and twirled until they were completely exhausted. In this trancelike state, participants felt that they could communicate with the gods. Music and dance had become forms of worship.

Other types of instruments began to appear by the time the first advanced civilizations arose in Mesopotamia (present-day Iraq) and Egypt, between 3000 B.C. and 2000 B.C. Stringed instruments, such as the harp and the lyre, were made by stretching animal tendons (fibrous tissue) across a wooden frame. Musicians plucked the strings with their fingers or with a pick to produce tones. Such instruments spread rapidly through the Mediterranean world and were also popular in India and China.

Wind instruments were also used in ancient times. People blew into large seashells and hollow reeds to create low, gentle sounds. Hollow animal horns were used to produce great blasts of sound, so they were useful for signals and communications over long distances as well as for making music. People developed a variety of wooden pipes and flutes of different lengths, with or without finger holes, including the Greek panpipes (named for the god Pan) and the Chinese bamboo flute.

Groups of musicians with string, wind, and percussion instruments came together to play at all manner of public gatherings, including religious ceremonies, weddings, hunting parties, and storytellings. Dancing almost always accompanied these gatherings. Performers danced in lines and in circles, alone and with partners. People often sang along as well—work songs, festival songs, HYMNS, and folktales.

In most ancient societies, almost everyone had some skill in music, song, and dance. They were a part of everyday life, and people were expected to join in. Young men in Greece were taught music and dance

Deadly Dancers

The ancient Greeks believed that good dancers were also good warriors. Because of this, young soldiers were expected to take dance lessons as part of their training. During some festivals in Athens, men and boys dressed in armor and performed dances in which they acted out battles.

Musicians and dancers often performed at banquets in ancient Egypt. This mural from an Egyptian tomb shows two young girls dancing to the music of a flute and hand clapping performed by four women musicians.

as part of their education, and the Olympic Games included competitions not only for athletes but also for singers, musicians, and dancers. Even the military society of the city-state of Sparta valued dance. Spartans knew that the best dancers—strong and agile—were also the best warriors.

In some cultures, music and dance developed into important forms of art. In Greece, for example, musicians accompanied recitals of poetry. Greek drama included musicians and a chorus, a group of performers who danced and sang as part of the play. In ancient India, highly trained dancers performed the *bharata natyam,* a complicated dance in which every hand movement and facial expression had a precise symbolic meaning.

The Romans were possibly the only ancient people who did not regard music and dance as a valuable part of daily life. Although they enjoyed these arts, they considered them unsuitable professions for a Roman citizen. Almost all dancers and musicians in Rome were foreigners or slaves. But outside Rome, in the empire's many provinces, music and dance continued to flourish among all classes of people. (See also *Feasts and Festivals; Literature.*)

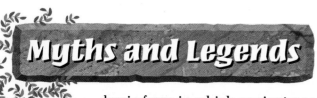 Myths and Legends

Myths and legends are the stories that a civilization tells about its gods, its heroes, and its history. Myths were the basic form in which ancient people expressed their understanding of the world. Because myths deal with important questions, such as how the universe began, they often involve SUPERNATURAL events. Legends, on the other hand, concern real people, events, and places, such as the deeds of great heroes, although certain aspects may be exaggerated.

Many myths served as a way to explain the mysterious workings of nature. For example, one Greek myth tells the story of Persephone, daughter of Demeter, the harvest goddess. Persephone was kidnapped by Hades, god of the underworld, who took her to be his queen. Sick with grief, Demeter refused to allow crops to grow on earth. The people begged the gods to find a solution. A compromise was arranged, in which Persephone would spend half the year with Hades and the other half with her mother. For the months Persephone spent with Hades, Demeter wept and refused to let plants grow. When Persephone returned, Demeter made the earth green again. This is how the Greeks explained the changing seasons—autumn, winter, spring, and summer.

Questioning the Myths

Not all Greeks accepted myths as true. The philosopher Plato believed that myths were merely stories that could be discussed while examining deeper philosophical issues. Plato's student Aristotle wrote harsh attacks on myths, claiming that they blocked the way to a true understanding of nature. Instead, he developed a scientific method based on logic and firsthand observation.

Historians are uncertain as to just how ancient peoples viewed such myths. The myths exist only as they were written down by various poets and playwrights, each of whom created his own version and added details as he pleased.

While some myths seem to explain events in nature, others were told for entertainment or moral education. The Roman poet Ovid popularized the story of Narcissus, a very handsome young man who fell in love with his own reflection in a pool of water. Narcissus lay by the water's edge, unable to tear himself away from his reflection, until he died on the spot. According to Ovid, the gods turned him into narcissus flowers, which often grow beside ponds and streams. The story warns against pride and vanity—*narcissist* is a modern word for someone who thinks only of himself or herself.

Legends range from amazing tales about heroes to grand retellings of history. One of the Greeks' most famous legends tells of Heracles (also called Hercules), the strongest man in the world. Heracles angered the goddess Hera, who drove him into a fit of insanity during which he killed his wife and children. To ATONE for these murders, Heracles had to perform 12 labors, all of which were considered impossible. His feats included killing a lion with his bare hands; slaying the Hydra, a nine-headed sea serpent; and capturing Cerberus, the fearsome three-headed watchdog of the underworld. Heracles succeeded in completing the 12 labors, and the gods rewarded his bravery by making him a god.

Historical legends included the EPIC poems of Homer and Virgil, in which they described the ancient histories of their people. Most Greeks and Romans knew these poems to be works of FICTION, but the tales still had a great influence on them. In shaping the world of the distant past, the societies that created myths and legends shaped their own lives. (See also *Aeneid; Literature; Muses; Rituals and Sacrifices.*)

The Sirens were mythological creatures whose beautiful songs caused sailors to go mad and crash their ships. The legendary hero Odysseus had his sailors' ears plugged, but had himself tied to the mast of his ship so that he could listen to the Sirens' song without endangering his life.

Nile River

The Nile is the longest river in the world. It begins in the lake region of central Africa, where it is called the White Nile. As it flows northward, the Nile gathers the waters of many smaller rivers, including the Blue Nile. By the time it nears Egypt, in North Africa, the Nile runs wide and deep.

The ancient civilization of Egypt developed in the valley of the Nile, sometime before 3100 B.C. The narrow valley of fertile land was surrounded by desert on both sides, confining human settlements to the river's banks. As the Nile wound northward through ancient Egypt, it passed Thebes, a powerful and wealthy city in southern Egypt.

Before the rise of Thebes, Egyptian pharaohs ruled from the city of Memphis, about 300 miles farther north. Just past Memphis, the Nile divides into many small streams as it spills into the Mediterranean Sea. Over thousands of years, the river has deposited tons of rich soil on Egypt's Mediterranean shore, forming a large, triangular region called a delta.

The Nile River played a major role in Egyptian life. Each year, as rains raised the water level, the river spilled over its banks, bringing water, minerals, and soil to nearby farms. If the river flooded too much or too little in a particular year, however, it harmed the crops and endangered the lives of many people. Because the entire cycle of Egyptian agriculture depended on the Nile, the river also influenced many aspects of religion, myth, and culture—it was the source of life, death, and renewal.

The Egyptians developed TECHNOLOGY to gain some control over the river. They dug canals to bring water to their fields. They built dams to keep water in reserve when the river returned to normal. Egyptian shipbuilders designed long, wide boats, or barges, that carried people and cargo up and down the river. By linking Egyptian cities and cultures, the Nile also helped the pharaohs rule Egypt as a single society. (See also *Agriculture.*)

During ancient times, the Nile River valley teemed with life. This mosaic shows some of the Nile's wildlife, including a hippopotamus, a crocodile, a cobra, a mongoose, and several ducks and other birds.

Olmecs

The Olmec civilization began around 1500 B.C., on the southern coast of the Gulf of Mexico. By 1200 B.C. the Olmec capital, located at a site now called San Lorenzo, had become a thriving center of culture, religion, trade, and government. Olmec influence spread across the highlands, rain forests, and coastal regions of Mexico and Central America.

One of San Lorenzo's most important features was an enormous hill of clay platforms on which houses and temples stood. The Olmecs built an elaborate system of stone drains that brought water through the city to collection pools.

Kings and priests exercised firm control over the people. The Olmec religion was

The Olmecs are famous for their gigantic stone sculptures of heads. Archaeologists believe the heads represent Olmec rulers.

strongly linked to nature. The jaguar appears in many Olmec sculptures, carvings, and mosaics. Some Olmec art shows figures called "were-jaguars," which are similar to werewolves—legendary monsters that are half human, half animal. Scholars believe that the were-jaguars reflect an Olmec belief that priests could transform the shape of their bodies.

Olmec religious art also included ceremonial weapons, such as axes, and small statues of rulers and heroes. These items were often made of blue and green jade, which were highly valued, and were often elaborately decorated with carvings and inscriptions. Some of these markings suggest that the Olmecs had begun to develop the HIEROGLYPHS used by the Maya civilizations that came later. Their stonework also included gigantic human heads—probably representing Olmec rulers. These sculptures measured as much as 9 feet tall and wide, and they weighed thousands of pounds.

Around 900 B.C., San Lorenzo declined in influence, and the center of Olmec power shifted eastward to another city, now called La Venta. Similar to the first capital city, La Venta had important buildings on clay platforms as well as a pyramid over 100 feet tall. This structure may have been built to resemble a volcano.

By 400 B.C. the Olmecs had completely abandoned San Lorenzo, and La Venta was in decline. The people of the region settled into several smaller, less powerful societies. However, many aspects of Olmec civilization were preserved in the great Mayan culture that soon arose in its place.

Olympic Games

The ancient Greek athletic festival called the Olympiad was held every four years. The Olympiad continued for more than 1,000 years, bringing together people from the far corners of the Greek world. These people gathered to honor the gods, to take a break from the almost constant wars, and to gain glory for themselves and for their communities.

The Olympiad took place in the city of Olympia in early autumn, after the summer crops had been harvested. Olympia was the central place of worship for the most important Greek god, Zeus, and the festival began as an occasion to celebrate his power. The ancient Greek poet Pindar suggested that another inspiration for the games was Heracles, or Hercules, the favorite hero of Greek legend. Heracles was the strongest man in Greece, and his superhuman feats earned him a place beside the gods.

Historians are not sure when the first Olympiad occurred, but the earliest records date from 776 B.C. Sports were not the only feature of the early games. Greeks also presented their dramatic, musical, and public-speaking skills. The festival included a single athletic event—a footrace across the stadium, which was about 600 feet long. The competition was for men only, and the first recorded winner was a cook named Coroibus. Gradually, the Greeks added races over longer distances as well as other events.

For many years, the ancient Olympic Games consisted of only one event—a footrace of about 200 yards called the stadion.

When the well-trained men of Sparta began to participate, the focus shifted to athletics. By 632 B.C. the games included running, jumping, wrestling, boxing, spear throwing, and horse and chariot racing. The festival lasted five days, and most of the competitors were either nobles or professional athletes. Each winner received a crown made of laurel branches. Along with the games, people enjoyed dances, feasts, and religious ceremonies. The final day ended with a parade for the champions.

When the great cities of Athens and Sparta sent their mightiest athletes to face one another, they brought their rivalries to the games. But during the Olympiad, the Greeks concentrated on sports, not on fighting. All participants agreed that there would be no warfare for several weeks before and after each Olympiad. This rule was to enable the athletes and spectators to travel to and from the games.

In 80 B.C. the games moved from Olympia to Rome, where they continued for more than 400 years. In A.D. 394, the Roman emperor Theodosius I ordered an end to the Olympic games. (See also *Feasts and Festivals; Gladiators; Oratory.*)

Marathon Man

In 490 B.C., the Greek city-state of Athens was fighting against the Persians in a fierce battle near the city of Marathon. The Athenians sent a man named Pheidippides to Sparta—a distance of about 125 miles—to ask for help. The runner arrived during a religious festival, so Spartan help never came. Pheidippides' heroism gave rise to the marathon—a 26-mile footrace that is part of the modern Olympic Games.

Oratory

The public and political life of ancient Greece and Rome was centered on oratory, the art of public speaking. To be persuasive public speakers, the Greeks and Romans studied rhetoric—the art of using words effectively in both writing and speaking.

The first teachers of rhetoric, called rhetoricians, may have been Corax and Tisias, both of whom lived in the Greek city-state of Syracuse. When the Syracusan ruler seized some private property, the owners asked Corax and Tisias to plead their case in court. Some people earned their living by writing speeches for others who needed to represent themselves in court.

Skill in oratory and rhetoric were also important in the assembly. The form of oratory most used in the assembly was debate. During a debate, speakers who represented opposing viewpoints presented their sides to the voters. Another type of oratory was the display speech. Usually given at public ceremonies or funerals, the display speech provided an opportunity for the speaker to show off his skills.

With political and legal issues at stake as well as personal reputations, orators studied hard to learn the methods of rhetoric. A speechwriter began by thinking of arguments and organizing them. The introduction might emphasize the speaker's good name and trustworthiness. The speaker would then state the facts and use reason to argue against any possible

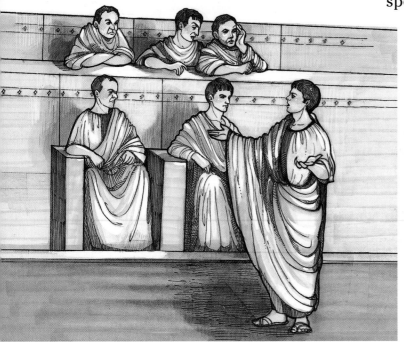

A Roman orator is shown here giving a speech before the Senate.

objections. The speech's conclusion was often a rousing appeal to the emotions of the audience.

The writer then worked on the style of the words and rhythms. The speaker learned ways to memorize the finished speech and to present it in public, using voice, body positions, and eyes to the greatest effect.

When the tradition of oratory passed to Rome, many of the finest speakers were the senators who governed the city. Great orators such as Cicero and Quintilian expanded on the rules and methods of rhetoric. They also pointed out that good speakers benefited from a sound education in a wide range of subjects. (See also *Democracy.*)

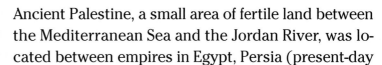
Palestine

Ancient Palestine, a small area of fertile land between the Mediterranean Sea and the Jordan River, was located between empires in Egypt, Persia (present-day Iran), and Mesopotamia (present-day Iraq). The region was often invaded by its more powerful neighbors. These invaders brought their customs, traditions, and religions to the region. Palestine is famous as the birthplace of two major religions of ancient times, Judaism and Christianity.

By 8000 B.C., Jericho, the first major walled city in Palestine, had been built. Other walled cities were built on the Mediterranean coast and in the mountains farther inland. By 3000 B.C., the people of these cities shared a similar culture. Historians refer to the people who lived in the region at this time as Canaanites and to their land as Canaan. Eventually the Canaanites began to fight among themselves, and this greatly weakened their city-states.

Between 1300 B.C. and 1100 B.C., Canaan suffered several invasions. The invaders, called Philistines, came by sea with organized armies and iron weapons. They seized control of the coastal cities. The word *Palestine* comes from the name of these people. Meanwhile, the Hebrew tribes arrived from the surrounding deserts, conquering the mountain settlements of Jericho and Jerusalem. The Philistines and Hebrews fought bitterly. In the 900s B.C. the Hebrews united under their kings—Saul, David, and Solomon—and defeated both the Philistines and the Canaanites.

The Hebrews formed two kingdoms, Israel and Judah. Many of them married Canaanites, adopting some Canaanite customs—including the language—in the process. Israel fell to the Assyrians in 722 B.C., and Judah fell to the Babylonians in 587 B.C. Even so, the Hebrews succeeded in preserving their religion, Judaism.

Although their land had been conquered, Canaanite culture survived in north Palestine among the Phoenicians. The Phoenicians were master sailors who had established trading colonies throughout the Mediterranean region—in North Africa, Sicily, and Spain.

Around 540 B.C., the entire region of Palestine came under Persian rule. The region was later ruled by other foreign powers, including Alexander the Great of Macedonia and the family of one of his generals, which became known as the Seleucid DYNASTY. The Jews of Palestine, led by a family of priests called the Maccabees, revolted against the Seleucids in 168 B.C. and established a new and independent Jewish kingdom. This kingdom lasted until 63 B.C., when Roman conquerors seized control. The Romans crushed another Jewish rebellion in A.D. 70, forcing the Jews to scatter throughout the vast Roman Empire. Palestine remained a Roman province and a Christian land until the Arabs invaded in A.D. 641.

Peloponnesian War

In 431 B.C. the Greek city-state of Sparta declared war on Athens, its chief rival. Tensions began when Athens established colonies and military bases throughout the eastern Mediterranean region, and its mighty navy often blocked food and other supplies from reaching other cities.

Athens suffered several major defeats but rebounded with a major victory in 410 B.C., destroying a Spartan navy and a Persian army.

Sparta turned the tide at last when its brilliant admiral, Lysander, built a navy that could challenge the Athenians. With support from Persia, Lysander blockaded the port of Athens. The Athenians held out for six months before hunger finally made them surrender in 404 B.C.

After the war, Sparta imposed harsh restrictions on the Athenian government. Within a few years the Athenians had restored their independence, their democracy, and their navy, but they never regained their former power and influence.

Pericles

Born around 495 B.C., Pericles entered public life as a lawyer and a member of the assembly of citizens that governed the new Athenian democracy.

Pericles' skillful speeches made him very popular among the people of Athens, and he soon became the most powerful man in the city. He made many important changes, including paying salaries to government officials. This arrangement enabled poorer citizens to serve. But he also changed the requirements for citizenship, limiting it to fewer people.

Pericles continued to build Athenian power. He transformed the Delian League—a loose alliance between Athens and its neighbors—into a powerful Athenian empire. He used the league's treasury to launch great building projects, including the Parthenon, a temple to the goddess Athena. Pericles was a great supporter of literature and the arts. During his 30-year rule, Athens was a lively city in which scholarship and the arts flourished.

But the growing power of Athens heightened tensions with Sparta and other Greek cities. In 431 B.C., Athens and Sparta went to war. Pericles commanded the Athenian military forces against Persians, Phoenicians, and other Greeks. Although he had important early victories, he was forced to accept a peace treaty with Sparta. Soon afterward a deadly disease broke out in the city, and Pericles was among the many who died. The renewed war with Sparta ended in defeat for Athens. (See also *Oratory; Peloponnesian War.*)

Persian Empire

The Persian Empire existed between 549 B.C. and 330 B.C. It was spread across a high, mountainous region in what is today Iran and Afghanistan. At the peak of its power and size, the Persian Empire was nearly as large as the present-day United States.

In about 1000 B.C., tribes called Iranians invaded the region from the north. One group of Iranians, the Medes, succeeded in establishing a kingdom around 700 B.C. But another group of Iranians, called the Parsa (or Persians), revolted against the Medes. The Persian leader, Cyrus the Great, created a new empire. He conquered Asia Minor, Babylon, and Palestine, then marched his armies eastward as far as India.

Emperor Darius I brought order to the empire and its borders. He established a system of government in which local governors called satraps managed their districts. As the empire became wealthy, Darius became a PATRON of art and architecture.

However, Darius encountered trouble with the Greeks. Cyrus had conquered several Greek-speaking cities on the west coast of Asia Minor. When these cities rebelled, Darius's armies returned to crush the revolts and then crossed the Aegean Sea to fight against the city-state of Athens on mainland Greece.

This glazed brickwork depicts one of the "10,000 Immortals," members of the Persian army. The name came from the practice of immediately replacing wounded or dead soldiers with new recruits in order to maintain the number of 10,000 soldiers.

The Athenians and their fellow Greeks defeated Darius. His son Xerxes I burned Athens in 480 B.C. but was defeated later that year at Thermopylae.

After this failure, the Persian Empire began to lose strength. The emperors were weak, and they faced many revolts in their own courts and throughout the vast empire. The last Persian emperor, Darius III, was defeated by Alexander the Great, king of Macedonia, in the 330s B.C.

For more than 550 years, foreign DYNASTIES ruled Persia. Beginning in the A.D. 200s, the Sassanian dynasty tried to restore the former glory of the Persian Empire. The dynasty's attempts to reconquer land brought it into conflict with the Romans. Although the Sassanians eventually lost all the territory they had seized from the Romans, they remained in control of Persia until about 650. (See also *Assyrian Empire*.)

Pharaohs

The pharaohs were the kings of ancient Egypt. According to legend, the first ruler of Egypt was the god Horus, who returned in the body of each succeeding pharaoh.

Egyptians believed that when a pharaoh died, his spirit left his body and traveled to the afterlife—the realm of the gods. As the power of the pharaohs grew, so did the size of their tombs. By 2500 B.C., pharaohs were laid to rest beneath huge stone pyramids, and their bodies were mummified. In the large underground chambers, detailed scenes of humans and gods covered the walls. The floors were lined with pottery, jewels, and sculptures. Temples, where priests continued to worship the pharaohs, were constructed around the pyramids.

Around 2180 B.C., Egypt entered a long period of civil war, during which people began to question the absolute power and authority of the pharaohs. It was also a time when much Egyptian land was taken over by the Hyksos, foreign invaders from Asia. During this so-called Middle Kingdom period, the pharaohs tried to regain their former godlike status.

Tutankhamen (King Tut) became pharaoh after this period. He died before he turned 20 and was not a very important ruler. When his tomb was discovered by ARCHAEOLOGISTS in A.D. 1922, however, the world marveled at the treasures within, including the royal coffin made of solid gold.

The kings of the next DYNASTY were called Rameses. The second of these rulers, Rameses II, ruled for more than 60 years. Historians believe that he is the pharaoh of the Bible who finally allowed the Jews to leave their enslavement in Egypt. After 1085 B.C., Egypt dissolved into many small kingdoms, and the rule of the pharaohs was replaced by foreigners. (See also *Cleopatra; Mummies; Nile River.*)

A Woman Pharaoh

The many remarkable pharaohs of ancient Egypt included one woman, Hatshepsut. She ruled in place of her young stepson. Her long reign was marked by peace and prosperity. However, she was bitterly resented by her stepson, and when she died in 1469 B.C., he ordered that all her statues and monuments be destroyed.

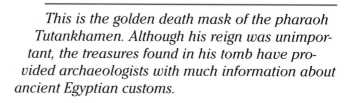

This is the golden death mask of the pharaoh Tutankhamen. Although his reign was unimportant, the treasures found in his tomb have provided archaeologists with much information about ancient Egyptian customs.

Eastern Philosophy

Philosophy, the study of ideas, developed rich and complex traditions in ancient India and China that still influence religions of the world. Eastern philosophers thought deeply about how people sense and understand the world around them.

Philosophy in India began with interpretations of the sacred texts of the Hindu religion. One of the oldest Hindu traditions was Samkhya, developed by Kapila in the 600s B.C. Kapila believed that people wanted to see and understand reality in its purest form but that they allowed too many differing personal viewpoints to interfere. Kapila taught that this interference led to discomfort and suffering.

The collection of Hindu ideas and beliefs known as Yoga tried to explain how a person could relieve suffering through meditation—a form of quiet, intense concentration. By clearing one's mind of the conflicting, false everyday world, a person could find true reality.

In the 400s B.C., a new religion, Buddhism, emerged to challenge Hinduism. Buddhist philosophers argued that there was no such thing as true reality. They suggested that since the universe was always changing, objects were unstable and unreal. All that existed was a person's understanding of the object, which was gained through sight, touch, and the other senses.

In China, early philosophers were more concerned with practical ways to live a good life. Mencius, a follower of Confucius, emphasized that human nature was basically good and that a government should teach goodness to its citizens. Xunzi, another Chinese thinker, disagreed, saying that people were evil and that a government had to force people to fulfill their duties.

This painting shows the legendary Chinese emperor Fu Hsi holding the symbol of yin and yang—the two basic principles of the universe. Yin and yang are opposites that go together in pairs—earth and sky, cold and warm, female and male.

These views were eventually challenged by Taoism, a philosophy and religion based on an idea called Tao, which means "the Way." Tao is considered neither real nor unreal but rather is seen as a creative process that Taoists try to understand and follow. (See also *Siddhartha Gautama*.)

Western Philosophy

The word *philosophy* means "love of wisdom" in Greek, and it refers to the study of ideas, including science. Greek thinkers studied and discussed many subjects, in four main categories—metaphysics, ethics, logic, and natural philosophy. Metaphysics seeks to learn what is true and real. Ethics deals with moral values and choices. Logic is a system of reasoning. And natural philosophy (now called science) examines the physical world.

The earliest Greek philosophers tried to understand how the universe was organized. In the 500s B.C., Thales of Miletus, sometimes called the father of philosophy, took the important step of rejecting myths and legends and seeking to understand the universe on his own.

This mosaic shows Plato surrounded by his students. Some historians consider Plato's school—the Academy—the world's first university.

Greek philosophers soon advanced many differing and strange ideas. Pythagoras, who lived in the late 500s and early 400s B.C., believed in a mystical harmony between the universe and mathematics. Empedocles, who lived in the 400s B.C., identified what he believed were the four universal elements—earth, air, fire, and water. Around the same time, Democritus proposed the existence of tiny particles called atoms.

In Athens, Socrates developed a method of dialogue, or conversation, in which he led people toward the ideas he favored by questioning their beliefs and encouraging them to reach their own conclusions. Socrates said "the unexamined life is not worth living."

Socrates' student Plato argued that societies needed kings who were also philosophers, guided by reason. To Plato, a state governed by philosopher-kings was a state that enjoyed harmony and justice. Plato had great concern for perfection, and he preferred ideals to real things.

Plato's student Aristotle, however, was much more curious about real things. He studied and wrote about many aspects of nature, politics, and the arts in a careful, scientific way. He also championed the use of LOGIC.

The Romans tried to apply Greek philosophy to their own lives and government. Cicero, a powerful senator and orator, thought that human laws should be based on the laws of nature. The growth of Christianity in the A.D. 300s led to a new tradition of Christian philosophers. (See also *Augustine; Philosophy, Eastern.*)

Poetry

Poetry began thousands of years ago in the words and rhythms of prayers, songs, and stories. However, poetry became a specific type of literature only after the invention of writing.

The earliest known poems were not written down until long after their creation. Many of these poems combined religion and history. The Egyptian Book of the Dead, written before 1000 B.C., describes death and the afterlife; it was intended to guide the souls of people who died. In the 900s B.C., Jewish poets composed HYMNS called psalms as well as the *Song of Solomon*, which deals with love between humans and God.

The Greek tradition of poetry began in the 700s B.C. with Homer's famous EPICS, the *Iliad* and the *Odyssey*. Over time, however, Greeks came to consider the epic form too long and rough. They valued shorter poems that better displayed a poet's skill and elegance. The poet Callimachus gained fame in the 200s B.C. for his witty love poems and hymns.

The Roman emperor Augustus enjoyed epics and may have encouraged his friend Virgil to produce the *Aeneid,* an epic about the founding of Rome. Shorter poetry also flourished in Rome, including the myths of Ovid, the wise instructions of Horace, and the love poems of Catullus.

Meanwhile, Chinese writers developed their own poetic tradition. The earliest Chinese poems, mostly folk songs and hymns, were written between 1000 and 600 B.C. and were collected in the *Book of Songs.* Many poetic forms flourished during China's great Han DYNASTY, from the 200s B.C. to the A.D. 200s. During that time, people had to show skill in writing poetry in order to serve in the government.

In the 400s B.C., poets in India began the *Mahabharata,* a collection of poems, myths, legends, and teachings about the ancient kingdoms of India and the Hindu god Vishnu. Many writers contributed to the *Mahabharata,* which took nearly 800 years to complete. (See also *Alphabets and Writing.*)

The Greek poet Homer influenced poetry in ancient Greece and inspired poets and writers throughout history.

The Poems of Sappho

The Greek poet Sappho wrote poems to honor Aphrodite, the goddess of love. Sappho included her most private thoughts and details in her poems. She was greatly admired by the philosopher Plato, who called her one of the Muses—the goddesses who inspired the arts. Most copies of her books were later destroyed by Christians who disapproved of her poems. Only one complete poem by Sappho exists today.

Rituals and Sacrifices

The word *ritual* refers to the specific order in which certain actions are performed and words are spoken as part of a religious ceremony. Rituals can range from short prayers to complicated dances and magic spells. Ancient societies included many rituals in their religious practices. The most important of these was the sacrifice, the offering of a gift to the gods.

Many early peoples practiced magic as a part of their religion. Often they prepared and sacrificed sacred objects in the belief that doing so would influence human behavior or the will of DEITIES. The magic worked only if the priest carefully followed every step of the ritual.

The same was true of most other religious practices. For example, the Egyptians had elaborate procedures for preparing a dead body for burial. They preserved the body with chemicals and bandages, recited certain prayers, and gathered special objects to accompany the body into the grave. Failure to conduct a proper burial, they thought, might mean that the soul would never reach the afterlife.

The Ritual of Beans

Some rituals had their basis in superstition—an unreasoning fear of something that is unknown or mysterious. The Romans held a yearly festival called Lemuria to expel ghosts from their households. At midnight the homeowner would walk through the house with nine black beans in his mouth, spitting them out for the ghosts to eat and saying, "With these beans I reclaim what is mine."

For many centuries, rituals played an important part in all aspects of Roman life, including war. Rome had 20 officials whose job was to conduct the appropriate rituals before fighting began. They would recite certain phrases and throw a special spear across the border into enemy territory. When peace returned, the Romans sacrificed a pig and declared that a curse would fall on Rome if the city's leaders broke the truce.

The sacrifices people offered to their gods might be as small as a few flowers or a bowl of rice. Sacrifices were serious events that required special rituals by priests to prepare the offering, the temple, and the altar. Specific rules guided the slaughter of the animals, the butchering and burning of the meat, and the eating of the meat by worshipers. Sometimes the priest might examine the animal's internal organs and use these observations to make predictions about the future. (See also *Mummies.*)

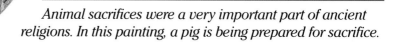

Animal sacrifices were a very important part of ancient religions. In this painting, a pig is being prepared for sacrifice.

Roads and Bridges

Travel in the ancient world developed with the construction of roads and bridges. Many early roads were built along routes that people had long traveled. Roads paved with stones appeared in Egypt, Mesopotamia, and India as early as 3000 B.C.

The Persians had a network of roads from at least the 500s B.C. Around that time they joined several existing roads into a great highway, known as the Royal Road. It was about 1,600 miles long. The Chinese emperor built a nationwide system that sped troops, traders, and postal messengers throughout the vast Chinese empire.

The Romans were the greatest ancient road builders. Because their empire was so vast, they needed to transport armies and government officials over great distances. The roads also made it easier for merchants and farmers to reach the city markets from the countryside. The Romans put great effort and expense into building and maintaining their roads.

Major Roman roads were marvels of engineering. Roman builders dug a smooth trench about three or four feet deep. They placed large rocks at the bottom, followed by smaller stones and cement, and topped with a layer of gravel or blocks of stone. They built the center slightly higher so that water drained toward the sides and collected in ditches. The Romans also made their roads as straight as possible, since the shortest distance between two points is a straight line.

Bridges were necessary wherever rivers or RAVINES prevented people from passing. Evidence suggests that bridges were built as early as 3500 B.C., with wood and stones laid across shallow streams or ropes suspended across canyons. Over time, engineers learned to arrange stones in arches, which could support huge weights. The Romans were as skilled at building bridges as they were with roads. They built sturdy stone posts in the currents of rivers to serve as the supports for a series of arches built across the river. A flat surface was then laid across the tops of the arches. (See also *Science and Technology; Transportation.*)

Roman roads were remarkably engineered so that they curved downward toward the sides, allowing excess rainwater to flow into ditches on either side of the road.

Rome

Over a period of 1,200 years, the city of Rome rose and fell. Growing from a small cluster of villages, it became the capital of one of the greatest empires the world has ever known. According to legend, Rome was founded after the ancient king Numitor lost his throne to his cruel brother Amulius. When Numitor's daughter gave birth to twin boys, Amulius ordered that the babies be drowned in the Tiber River. Instead, servants set them adrift in a basket. A wolf found them and fed them, and a shepherd and his wife then raised the boys, naming them Romulus and Remus.

When the twins grew up, they restored their grandfather to the throne. They decided to build a city at the place where the wolf had found them. However, they argued about who should be king of the new city. Romulus killed Remus and built Rome on one of seven hills in the region.

Historians doubt the legend of Rome's creation. They believe that the city grew from a number of small villages. Around 700 B.C. these villages united and established the Roman Forum as a central meeting place and market. At first Rome was ruled by kings, and it became a large and prosperous city. Rome's last king, Tarquin the Proud, was overthrown in 510 B.C., and the Romans established a republic—a government in which they elected officials called senators to represent them and govern according to law.

Most of the senators were wealthy Romans, called patricians. This angered the other Roman citizens, called plebeians. The plebeians demanded more power, and in 474 B.C. they elected leaders to their own assembly, which they called the *Concilium Plebis.* The plebeians gained some rights, but the patricians still controlled Roman politics.

In 146 B.C., Rome conquered Greece. This and other victories brought enormous wealth and territory to Rome's upper classes, but tensions over land ownership and military service led to more unrest among the plebeians.

During the 130s and 120s B.C., two plebeian brothers—Tiberius and Gaius Gracchus—tried to establish reforms to aid ordinary citizens. Although both brothers were assassinated, they had already begun a movement in the Senate to remove some of the privileges of the upper classes. This movement led to a period of civil war and to the rise of military dictatorships.

In 60 B.C., three generals—Julius Caesar, Crassus, and Pompey—formed an alliance to take over the government. Eleven years later, after Crassus had died and Pompey had been defeated, Caesar seized control of the republic. He was

Map of Rome

In 1998, archaeologists uncovered a 2,000-year-old fresco map of the city. On this extraordinary mural, the artist had painted buildings reflected on the water, as if the painter had been looking at the city from above. Excitement over this find ran high, and the Italian government has set aside about $300 million to pay for additional excavations in Rome.

immensely popular with the common people, but not with the senators. Fearing that Caesar was gaining too much power, a group of senators murdered him in 44 B.C. Caesar's death touched off a new struggle for power, this time between Octavian (Caesar's grandnephew) and Mark Antony (Caesar's friend). Octavian won, and his rise to power in 31 B.C. marked the end of the Roman Republic and the beginning of the Roman Empire.

According to legend, the babies Romulus and Remus were abandoned in the wilderness. There they were nursed by a she-wolf until a kind shepherd found them and raised them.

To show the Senate that he did not intend to be a dictator, Octavian pretended to share power with the senators and other officials. The Senate rewarded Octavian by naming him Augustus, which means "revered" or "honored." As the first emperor of Rome, Augustus reorganized the army and added vast amounts of territory to the empire. His reign began a long time of prosperity that came to be called the Pax Romana, which means "Roman peace." His death in A.D. 14 was followed by two DYNASTIES—the Julio-Claudian and the Antonine emperors, who ruled for almost 200 years.

The empire nearly collapsed in the 200s as Roman armies struggled to hold the borders against the Persians in the east and Germanic tribes from the north. Dozens of emperors rose and fell in a series of power struggles. As Rome's political and economic power declined, a new religion—Christianity—emerged. Fearing the growing appeal of Christianity, the emperors fought bitterly to destroy it.

By the late 300s, the empire had been divided into the Western Roman Empire, with its capital in Rome, and the Eastern Roman Empire, with its capital in Constantinople. The eastern rulers stood by while Germanic and Asian tribes trampled the vulnerable Western Empire and looted Rome in 410 and 455. The German leader Odoacer forced the last emperor of the Western Empire, Romulus Augustulus, to give up the throne in 476.

Although Rome entered a period of neglect and ruin, the influence of its laws, science, and culture never truly faded. Roman law became the basis for several legal systems in Western Europe. Latin—the language of the Romans—developed into French, Italian, and Spanish. (See also *Aeneid; Attila the Hun; Carthage; Democracy.*)

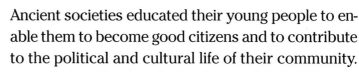
Schools

Ancient societies educated their young people to enable them to become good citizens and to contribute to the political and cultural life of their community. Most young people learned what they needed to know while working in the fields or as assistants to master craftsmen. Education in reading, writing, music, and literature was a luxury available only to nobles or other wealthy families, who could afford to hire private tutors for their children.

Some of the first schools were established in Egypt around 3000 B.C. These schools existed in temples, where priests taught young people how to read and write. Students who successfully completed their education often became SCRIBES or priests. However, education was available only to children of nobles, and only a few boys and even fewer girls were taught.

In the 400s B.C. the Greek city-state of Athens made education available to all citizens. However, citizenship was denied to women and slaves, who made up more than half the region's population. The children of Athenian citizens learned gymnastics, music, dance, poetry, reading, writing, and mathematics. Parents paid fees to the teachers, who were free men assisted by slaves. Students could be hit with a cane if they disobeyed the teacher, but they could also win awards when they displayed their knowledge successfully in public competitions.

More advanced education in Greece began during the 300s B.C., when the PHILOSOPHER Plato founded the Academy, the first institute of higher learning. He and his students gathered in small groups to discuss issues of PHILOSOPHY and politics. Plato's student Aristotle later founded his own school, the Lyceum. Aristotle spent less time on discussion and more time on scientific investigation and observation.

The Roman government opened public schools around A.D. 100. Unlike the Greeks, the Romans provided education for both girls and boys. From the age of six or seven, children learned reading, writing, and mathematics. Romans did not value music and dance as highly as the Greeks did. Also, they studied literature not for its beauty but as a guide to history and proper behavior. Many of the teachers in Rome were Greek.

Greek boys were often accompanied to school by a slave called a pedagogue. He is shown here waiting as the boy recites his lessons to the teacher.

Science and Technology

Most ancient peoples did not practice science in the modern sense of THEORIES, experiments, and proofs. Instead they carefully observed the natural events that occurred around them, such as the rising and setting of the sun and the opening of a flower's petals in the morning. Gradually they learned to use their observations to create TECHNOLOGY—tools, machines, and methods—that helped them shape the world to fit their needs.

One of the first observations people made was of the movement of stars and other bodies in the sky. Eventually people began to recognize patterns and cycles in these movements, which enabled them to predict accurately when a certain star could be seen in a particular place in the sky.

Ancient people also observed that strong, healthy animals usually gave birth to strong, healthy offspring. This knowledge of BIOLOGY enabled people to breed animals with desired characteristics. People also applied their scientific knowledge to farming, planting seeds from the most fruitful plants in order to increase their harvests.

The Greeks were the first known scientists to believe that natural events could be understood through careful observation and LOGIC. Hippocrates, a Greek physician who lived around 400 B.C., was the first to teach that illness was the result of natural causes, not the will of the gods.

The wealth and stability of Greek civilization enabled its scientists to consider questions simply for the sake of learning, rather than to solve everyday problems. For example, during the 200s B.C., Aristarchus of Samos proposed that all the planets, including the earth, revolved around the sun. Aristarchus was correct, but his theory did not affect the lives of ordinary Greeks.

The Romans collected and organized the scientific knowledge of other peoples. They were, however, highly skilled in the use of that knowledge, especially to engineer elaborate structures. Roman roads, bridges, ships, and buildings surpassed all others in the ancient world. (See also *Architecture; Astronomy and Astrology; Mathematics; Medicine.*)

Aqueducts enabled Romans to channel millions of gallons of water a day to cities miles away from the water's source. This ancient Roman aqueduct, the Pont du Gard, still stands in France.

Seven Wonders of the Ancient World

The architects, engineers, and sculptors of the ancient world produced some the largest and most extraordinary structures in history. Seven of these became known as the Wonders of the Ancient World. People visited these sites in great numbers to marvel at their grandeur, but most of these wonders were destroyed by war, neglect, or natural disasters.

The pyramids of Egypt were by far the oldest and largest of the wonders. They were built between 2600 B.C. and 1800 B.C. at Giza and Saqqara, outside the ancient Egyptian capital of Memphis. These enormous stone structures served as royal tombs for the pharaohs, symbolizing their rising to the heavens. The largest still stands more than 750 feet high. Even when Egypt became a Greek territory, and later a Roman one, the pyramids stood as a reminder of Egypt's glory. Of all seven wonders, only the pyramids still exist.

The Hanging Gardens of Babylon displayed only a fraction of the city's dazzling wealth under its king Nebuchadnezzar II in the 500s B.C. This arrangement of trees, flowers, and plants covered a 23-foot-high wall of the palace. Citizens entering the city could see the gardens high above the Ishtar Gate, which was itself an impressive sight, covered in carvings of bulls and dragons coated in blue glaze. According to legend, the king built the gardens to remind his wife of her home in the mountains. The gardens apparently withered when Babylon's power declined.

The people of Ephesus, in Greece, built the Temple of Artemis around 560 B.C. to honor the goddess of hunting, wild animals, and children. The temple had an open roof, tall columns, and wall carvings of mythical scenes. Destroyed by fire in 356 B.C., the temple was rebuilt by the people of Ephesus and the neighboring states. The temple fell again when the Goths, a tribe from the north, invaded Ephesus in A.D. 263.

The lighthouse on an island in Alexandria harbor stood more than 400 feet high. It guided ships for 1,500 years until it was destroyed in an earthquake.

In the 430s B.C. the Greek city of Olympia hired the famous Athenian sculptor Phidias to build a statue of Zeus, the chief Greek god. Nearly 40 feet high and made of gold and ivory, the figure of Zeus sat majestically on a throne richly decorated with ebony, glass, and precious jewels. Much later, the emperor Theodorus I had the statue brought to Constantinople, where it was destroyed by fire in A.D. 475.

The fifth wonder was the tomb of Mausolus, a Persian governor of the Greek city Halicarnassus. When he died around 350 B.C., his wife, Artemisia, honored him with a magnificent marble tomb built to resemble a temple. Sculpted lions surrounded the building's massive base, and a chariot stood on the 24-step pyramid that made up its roof. This great monument, known as the Mausoleum, was destroyed by an earthquake sometime before the 1400s. It is from this monument that we get the modern word *mausoleum,* which refers to any large tomb.

The sixth wonder, the Colossus of Rhodes, was a statue of the sun god Helios. It was built around 280 B.C. on the Greek island of Rhodes to celebrate a victory over Macedonia. Looking out to sea from the island's harbor, the shining bronze god stood more than 100 feet tall, his head crowned by the sun's rays. After just a few decades, an earthquake struck the island. The Colossus broke at the knees and fell to the ground.

The last of the Seven Wonders is the Pharos of Alexandria, a lighthouse at the city's port. Built around 280 B.C., the lighthouse towered 400 feet above the harbor. Large mirrors at the top reflected the light from a fire that was kept burning inside the structure. The light could be seen for many miles out to sea. The lighthouse survived for about 1,500 years.

Ships and Shipbuilding

Throughout history, people have used boats and ships for travel, trade, and war. The earliest boats were probably canoes made of hollow trees, or rafts made from bundles of reeds, twigs, and grasses tied together. The first sailing ship would have been a raft with a single mast and a square sail.

The ancient Egyptians possessed excellent shipbuilding skills. The funeral boat for the pharaoh Cheops, who died in 3908 B.C., was 133 feet long and 26 feet wide and was made of wood. Such ships, called galleys, were rowed by large teams of slaves.

The Phoenicians improved the galley's design after 1000 B.C. The basic principles of Phoenician shipbuilding included a long wooden keel that ran the length of the boat's bottom like a backbone, shorter ribs running from side to side, and wooden planks that formed the open hull. The ships were held together by wooden pegs or iron nails and were coated with tar to make them waterproof. Sails, usually made of cloth, featured colorful dyes and decorations. With such ships, the Phoenicians became some of the greatest merchant sailors of the ancient world.

Mediterranean merchant ships usually relied on sails because oarsmen took up valuable cargo space. Merchants often chose ships with taller sides to increase the amount of cargo they could carry. By the 100s B.C., Roman cargo ships could carry as much as 400 tons.

Greek warships had up to three levels of oarsmen on each side; the Romans had five levels. Warships often had ramming devices at the prow (the front of the ship) to pierce the sides of enemy vessels.

Other cultures developed their own styles of shipbuilding. The Chinese built ships known as junks with wooden decks laid over hulls that were made of two canoes lashed together. Meanwhile, Arabs and Indians set sail in ships called dhows, with triangular sails that later influenced shipbuilding designs. (See also *Transportation.*)

To avoid being rammed by enemy ships, ancient warships were built for speed and mobility. Roman warships are shown here.

Siddhartha Gautama, born around 560 B.C., was a prince in northern India. He founded the religion of Buddhism. According to tradition, Siddhartha's birth had been predicted by an ancient PROPHET. The man told Siddhartha's father, the king, that the baby would become either a great king or a very wise man. Hoping that his son would succeed him on the throne, the king tried to limit his son's experiences. The prince lived a sheltered life of pleasure and was married when he was only 16.

One day Siddhartha decided to tour the countryside in his chariot. Shocked to find great poverty and suffering among the people, he decided to abandon his life of luxury. At age 29 he left his wife and young son and traveled as a beggar for several years, searching for teachers who would guide him.

Unable to find the knowledge he sought, he decided to stop and meditate under a tree until true wisdom came to him. He sat there all night, and by dawn he had come to a new understanding of how a person could live a life that was a middle ground between luxury and poverty. He then took on students and spread his wisdom.

Buddha's most basic teachings are called the Four Noble Truths. The first truth is that suffering exists in a world that is always changing. The second is that suffering has causes. The third is that a person can break the chain of events that causes suffering. When a person escapes suffering, he or she reaches a state of complete peace and wisdom called nirvana. The fourth truth is that a person can reach nirvana by following a path that includes discipline, MEDITATION, and faith.

The Buddha taught for many years. After his death in 480 B.C., his students continued his teachings and worshiped at the places that had been important in his life, such as the tree where he had reached enlightenment. (See also *Hinduism.*)

This painting shows Siddhartha Gautama (Buddha) meeting an elderly man, a sick man, a dead man, and a religious man. Encounters such as these led Siddhartha to follow a religious life and search for an end to human suffering.

Slaves and Slavery

Slavery—the ownership of one person by another—was common and almost unquestioned in every ancient society. Before 2000 B.C., the Mesopotamian city-state of Sumer had laws concerning the treatment of slaves. In Sumerian writing, the symbol for slave was similar to that for foreigner. Indeed, few societies ever enslaved members of their own ethnic, social, or tribal groups. Most slaves were people captured during invasions and wars—not only soldiers but sometimes entire civilian populations.

Some ancient societies granted limited rights to their slaves. In Babylon, the Code of Hammurabi stated that slaves could own property, start businesses, and marry free people. However, slaves could still be bought or sold at any time. In most ancient societies, slaves who earned wages could eventually purchase their freedom from their owners. Although some people spoke out against the harsh treatment of slaves, none suggested that slavery should be abolished.

Ancient Egypt depended heavily on slaves to work on farms and for large construction projects, such as the pyramids. The Egyptians also had debt slavery, in which a man could sell himself or his wife and children in order to pay his debts.

Ancient Greece and Rome were also slave-owning societies. The Athenian statesman Solon ended debt slavery in the 500s B.C., but this only increased the demand for slaves in the fields, pastures, and mines. Slave markets thrived in Athens, Rhodes, Corinth, and other major cities, where 1,000 slaves might be traded in a single day. By the time the reign of the Roman emperor Augustus began in 31 B.C., more than 2 million slaves worked in Italy, mostly on large farms owned by wealthy nobles. (See also *Gladiators.*)

The workers shown in this ancient Egyptian drawing were either slaves or paid laborers. Both classes worked on large construction projects, such as the pyramids.

King Solomon

Solomon, the third king of ancient Israel, began his rule around 961 B.C. He strengthened the stability of his kingdom by dividing it into 12 districts, each governed by a deputy. Each district was responsible for supplying the court with food and other supplies for one month of the year. Solomon also secured the borders of his country and established trade between Israel and Phoenicia.

After securing peace in his realm, Solomon launched several ambitious building projects. He ordered the construction of a large stone temple in the capital city, Jerusalem. Tensions rose in Israel toward the end of Solomon's long reign. The people resented the forced labor and heavy taxes that the construction required. After Solomon's death in 922 B.C., his son Rehoboam refused to lighten these burdens on the people. (See also *Palestine.*)

The Real Mother

The wisdom of Solomon is described in a biblical story in which two women claimed to be the mother of the same baby. Since neither woman would give up her claim to the child, Solomon said he would cut the baby in two with his sword and give each woman half. As the king raised his sword, one woman cried out, "Give the baby to her." Solomon recognized this concerned woman as the baby's true mother.

Sparta

The ancient Greek city of Sparta was founded in the 800s B.C. by the Dorians. Sparta rose to power by invading the lands of Messenia and Laconia and enslaving the people, who became known as helots. Sparta's political stability was threatened after 669 B.C., when the helots launched a fierce rebellion. The fighting continued for years.

When the Spartans had put down the revolt, they reorganized the country into a tightly controlled military state. The government gave every male citizen a plot of land, and in return, each citizen served for a time as a professional soldier. Children were taken from their families when they were about seven years old and raised in military training camps.

As a major military power, Sparta took the lead in defending Greece in the wars against the Persian Empire in the 480s B.C. After the Persian Wars, tensions rose between Sparta and Athens, resulting in the Peloponnesian War in 431 B.C. Persia came to the aid of Sparta, and after years of bitter fighting, Athens was defeated in 404 B.C.

Although victorious, Sparta had been greatly weakened by an earthquake and another helot rebellion. In 371 B.C. the city of Thebes forced Sparta to surrender the Messenian lands and the helots. Of Sparta's 1,200 remaining citizens, 400 died in battle, and the city never regained its former might.

Trade

In early human societies, families and communities produced most of the food and materials they needed. Later, villages became cities and their populations grew, and trade—the exchange of goods and services—became one of the most widespread human activities.

With the development of writing and record keeping, city-states developed complex economies. The people of a region sold their surplus goods to foreigners and purchased the goods they could not provide for themselves. Trade also encouraged the spread of culture, knowledge, and religion as merchants from many places met and mingled in busy markets.

Sometimes hundreds of traders gathered with thousands of pack animals and traveled together by land. These groups, called caravans, traveled many ancient trade routes. Among the most famous trade routes was the Silk Road. It stretched from Persia (present-day Iran) to China. The name came from the highly prized fabric—silk—that was brought from China.

However, travel by water was much cheaper and faster than travel by land. Ships hauled cargo between the hundreds of ports and harbors in the ancient world. As early as 3000 B.C., merchants from Egypt sailed for East Africa, returning with ships full of gold and slaves. The warm, calm waters of the Indian Ocean enabled merchants to sail among the ports in Africa, the Middle East, India, and East Asia. Like the Silk Road, these routes brought highly valued goods, such as spices and silk cloth, to the Mediterranean region.

Trade in the Mediterranean grew after 1000 B.C., led by the skillful

Pirates on the Seas

Piracy was a major threat to merchants and travelers throughout the ancient world. Although Roman law provided harsh punishments for pirates, including beheading, piracy continued. In 67 B.C. the Roman general Pompey crushed several pirate fleets, and the Romans were able to keep the Mediterranean safe from pirates for about 150 years.

sailors of Phoenicia. From their homeland in Palestine, the Phoenicians built colonies along the Mediterranean coast where they traded goods, repaired their ships, and stored goods for future deliveries. The Phoenician capitals of Tyre and Sidon were famous for products such as cedar wood and Tyrian purple, a dye so bright and so expensive that it became the color worn by the Roman emperors.

The Greeks, who learned much from the Phoenicians, also founded many colonies in the Mediterranean. By the late 600s B.C., trade increased as people began to use money for payment instead of merely exchanging goods.

The city-state of Athens used its powerful navy to protect its commerce. From its bustling port, Piraeus, Athenians sold large amounts of wine, olives, oil, and silver, while bringing in grain, wood, spices, iron, gold, and copper. Like many cities, Athens actively controlled the flow of goods, often charging foreign traders a tax to sell their products in Athenian markets.

Rome far surpassed Athens as a center of trade. At its port in Ostia, Romans imported vast quantities of food and raw materials, often sent by conquered peoples to pay the heavy taxes imposed on them by Rome. Roman trade was so intense that major cities such as Carthage (in present-day Tunisia) and Alexandria (in Egypt) served as warehouses for goods going to and from Rome. After the Roman Empire fell in A.D. 476, trade in the region declined as well. (See also *Agriculture; Ships and Shipbuilding; Slaves and Slavery; Transportation.*)

Cargo ships hauled tons of goods among hundreds of ports and harbors. The Phoenicians were among the most highly skilled sailors in the ancient world.

Transportation

Transportation includes all of the means by which people and goods move or are moved from one place to another. In the ancient world, travel by land usually meant walking and carrying one's own possessions. Eventually people learned to train animals, such as camels, mules, dogs, oxen, and horses, to carry or pull their loads.

Around 3500 B.C., people in Mesopotamia invented the wheel and built the first wheeled vehicles. The most common vehicles—two-wheeled carts and four-wheeled wagons—increased the amounts of goods or baggage that people could transport.

The invention of the wheel inspired societies to build new roads, because carts and wagons needed wide roadways and smooth surfaces. Even on the well-built Roman roads (laid out more than 3,000 years later), wagons were terribly noisy and unstable. Still, armies, farmers, traders, and other travelers could not hope for better.

Since land travel was slow and difficult, most people preferred to travel by water. Ships and boats offered the quickest and cheapest way to transport armies or large cargoes. Merchants and dockworkers developed efficient methods for storing and loading goods, and Roman ships could carry several hundred tons.

Water transportation had its disadvantages and dangers, however. To avoid stormy seas, ships normally traveled only in late spring, summer, and early fall. They sailed in winter only in times of emergency, such as war or famine. Even in summer, ships depended on favorable winds to catch the sails and propel the ship forward. Without sails, a ship needed dozens of men to row it. Merchants faced the added risk of losing their cargoes to pirates.

No seagoing vessels were designed as passenger ships. People who wanted to travel by sea had to go to the port and look for a cargo vessel headed for their destination. The passengers had to pay the ship's captain and bring their own food and bedding. Those who could not pay had the option of becoming sailors and earning their way. (See also *Roads and Bridges; Ships and Shipbuilding; Trade.*)

This gold coin from the 300s B.C. shows one of the best known means of transportation in the ancient world—the chariot.

Trojan War

In Greek legend and literature, Greek armies are said to have crossed the Aegean Sea to wage a ten-year war against the city of Troy. Historians believe that such a struggle may have occurred around 1200 B.C., but no actual historical account exists. The story is best known from Homer's EPIC the *Iliad,* which was written more than 400 years later.

According to legend, the Trojan War erupted because Paris, a prince of Troy, fell in love with Helen, the wife of King Menelaus of Sparta. Paris took Helen to Troy, arousing her husband's anger. Menelaus then rallied several Greek cities to his cause. The Greek armies, led by Menelaus's brother Agamemnon, surrounded Troy and demanded the return of Helen. Priam, the king of Troy, refused.

For ten years the opposing forces battled on the fields of Troy. Then, according to Homer, trouble flared up among the Greeks. Agamemnon captured the daughter of a Trojan priest and refused to return her. The Greek hero Achilles demanded the girl as his own and when Agamemnon refused, Achilles declared he would no longer fight the Trojans.

Without the great warrior Achilles, the Greeks were no match for the Trojans and their leader Hector (Priam's son). Achilles' closest friend, Patroclus, was killed by Hector. Achilles returned to the field, and

According to legend, Greek soldiers hid inside an enormous wooden horse and tricked the Trojans into bringing it into Troy. This sculpture shows the Greek soldiers hiding inside the famous Trojan Horse.

he slew Hector in a fierce duel. He dragged Hector's body around the city until Priam humbly pleaded for the return of his son for a proper funeral. Achilles, who felt compassion and admiration for Priam, released the body. But Achilles himself died soon after, struck by an arrow shot from the bow of Paris.

The Greeks tried one last cunning strategy. They pretended to retreat from Troy, leaving behind a gigantic wooden horse as a gift. The curious Trojans brought the horse within the city walls. When night fell, Greek soldiers came out from their hiding place inside the Trojan horse. They opened the city's gates to the Greek army, which burst in and defeated the Trojans in a bloody battle. (See also *Helen of Troy; Virgil.*)

Underworld

Many ancient religions believed in life after death. Usually souls went to the underworld, a mysterious kingdom of the dead.

In Greek mythology, both the underworld and the god who ruled there were called Hades. After death, the soul was carried across the mythical river Styx by Charon, the boatman. The Greeks often buried dead relatives with coins in their mouths to pay Charon's fee. Once inside Hades, souls came before judges who examined their past lives. Those who had committed minor sins might be sentenced to wander the underworld forever. Worse offenders could expect torture, labor, hunger, and disease. Virtuous souls were sent from Hades to the faraway Island of the Blessed, also called the Elysian fields.

This Greek vase painting shows Persephone and Hades in their palace in the underworld.

The Romans knew the god Hades by the name of Pluto. According to the poet Virgil, most souls simply remained in the underworld, neither happy nor suffering. By A.D. 200, the Roman concept of the underworld began to give way to the Christian ideas of heaven and hell. (See also *Mummies; Myths and Legends.*)

Virgil

The Roman poet Virgil was born in 70 B.C. in a small village in the north of Italy. His first work, the *Eclogues,* appeared in 36 B.C. These ten poems describe the joys and hardships of farmers and shepherds in the countryside. Virgil asks his readers whether poetry can have value when suffering exists in the world. Virgil won much honor and admiration for his poems, especially from the Roman leader Octavian.

Virgil moved to the southern city of Naples, where he produced his second work, the *Georgics.* These four poems give instruction in the skills of farming while discussing issues of death, time, and war. Romans praised Virgil's moving descriptions of rural life and the beauty of his writing style.

Octavian, who had become the emperor Augustus, SPONSORED Virgil's next work, the *Aeneid.* This EPIC poem tells the story of Aeneas, a hero of the Trojan War, and of the origins of the Roman people. The *Aeneid* was still unfinished when Virgil died in 19 B.C. He had ordered that his papers be burned, but Augustus overruled that wish. (See also *Homer.*)

106